LUNCHLADIES
BOUGHT MY
PROM DRESS

A MEMOIR

LUNCHLADIES BOUGHT MY PROM DRESS

A MEMOIR

HEATHER REAM

KHAMIA PRESS

Knoxville, Tennessee

For information about this title or to order other books and/or electronic
media, contact the publisher:

Hkamia Press
heatherream.com

Cover and interior design by The Book Cover Whisperer:
OpenBookDesign.biz

Publisher's Cataloging-in-Publication data

Names: Ream, Heather, author.
Title: Lunchladies bought my prom dress / by Heather Ream.
Description: Knoxville, TN: Hkamia Press, 2023.
Identifiers: LCCN: 2023907913 | ISBN: 979-8-9882357-0-5 (paperback) |
979-8-9882357-1-2 (ebook) Subjects: LCSH Ream, Heather. | Poor--
United States--Biography. | Poor children--United States--Biography.
| Knoxville (Tenn.)--Biography. | Children of clergy--United States--
Biography. | BISAC BIOGRAPHY & AUTOBIOGRAPHY / Personal
Memoirs Classification: LCC HV741 .R43 2023 | DDC 362.7092--dc23

Library of Congress Control Number: 2023907913

979-8-9882357-0-5 Paperback
979-8-9882357-1-2 eBook

Printed in the United States of America

FIRST EDITION

For my sister, Rebekah, who held my hand
so I wouldn't walk the rocky path alone.

CONTENTS

IN THE BEGINNING

As a young woman, Mama hated going on dates. Although a few boys were considerate, respecting Mama's boundaries despite her irresistible pocket doll petiteness and auburn curls, they were in the minority.

"Most of them couldn't keep their hands to themselves. And I ought to know. I went to seminary," she told me early on, exposing me to the reality of concupiscent Baptist preachers long before any of them were on TV crying confessionally over extramarital affairs.

Mama had graduated from college with a degree in early childhood education. Convinced the Lord wanted her to continue her learning, she moved from Arkansas to Fort Worth, Texas, to attend their big Baptist seminary. Although she was a born talker and as enthusiastic about Jesus as a coliseum full of Billy Grahams, her path would not lead to preaching. Even if the seminary allowed women to preach – which they didn't

– the advisors felt Mama's sweet, yet impetuous, nature was better suited to children's ministry than church leadership.

Unofficially, the only program options for women were either children's ministry or husband procurement. Children's ministry was her preference by far. Having grown up on a farm, Mama was familiar with many kinds of husbandry. If she was expected to rear a helpless creature, she at least wanted a steady paycheck to go with it.

Daddy was a musical prodigy. By age 14, he was an accomplished fiddler playing gigs booked by my papaw, who was still recovering from his own brush with fame as a musician. As a boy, Daddy shared the stage with many of country music's greats but still dutifully handed my mammaw his paycheck after every event. Daddy, tall for his age, sometimes had to drive home after shows because Papaw got too drunk to get back safely. Feeling the weight of responsibility on his young shoulders, Daddy began to hate the performances, the practice, and the pressure. He quit playing the fiddle forever.

College did not interest Daddy. After high school, he gigged with a few local rock and roll bands before beginning work for a gospel radio station in town. Daddy was a gentle and genuine man of faith and well-suited for Christian broadcasting. He enjoyed being an announcer, encouraging listeners with Scripture and uplifting commentary. It was a silver lining to all those years of performing.

Daddy became friends with a pastor who preached on air daily at the station. Recognizing Daddy's bona fide beliefs and talent for entertaining the masses, the pastor encouraged him to attend his alma mater, the Baptist seminary in Fort Worth.

Daddy had been in plenty of churches and plenty of venues. Whether glass-eyed from religious fervor or glass-eyed from cheap whiskey, audiences pretty much looked the same. Both groups seemed to like him. Deciding to go for it, he loaded up his tiny blue convertible and hit the road.

↝

"MAY I WALK YOU ladies to class?" asked Daddy one fine September morning. He had been waiting in front of the women's dorm for what seemed like forever, ready to escort. Mama's girlfriends tittered appreciatively, but Mama ignored him. She was instead focused on her highly flammable hairdo. It had been sprayed into submission, and she was praying it wouldn't burst into flames. The Texas heat was already oppressive, reminiscent of hellfire, and perfect for a Baptist seminary.

The handsome young man, new this semester, had been walking with them since the first day of classes. Mama was sure he was hanging around because he was interested in her friend, a lovely girl whose demure nature was perfect for winning souls and gazing adoringly at a future husband.

In fact, everything about the girl seemed perfect to Mama, especially the delicate gold cross necklace that enhanced her swanlike loveliness.

Mama had grown up a tomboy and was about as demure as a carnival barker selling health tonic. She could never be the kind of wife that would rear children in a dignified manner or cook dinner without comment, like her friend or the bevy of Baptist beauties who swarmed the seminary.

This was Mama's second year on campus, and she reminded herself she was there to learn about children's ministry, anyway. Being fair and honest before the Lord, however, Mama also noted that while her friend's necklace complemented her neck, it did nothing for her flat bosom.

Mama did not have such a problem, praise God.

She followed her girlfriends across the quad, half listening to their chatter as they approached their respective buildings. Mama was grateful her hairdo was still intact as she opened the door. Daddy followed her all the way to her classroom.

"Would you like to go for a walk later, just the two of us?" he asked.

"You wanna go on a walk with *me*?" Mama replied, more annoyed than incredulous.

Taken aback, Daddy stammered, "I think so."

Mama considered it. He was handsome, this tall guy with kind brown eyes, but she knew exactly how this would end.

She had seen plenty of guys act like angels during convocation but horned devils at the drive-in.

Still, he seemed decent, and it was always nice to be wanted. She figured there was no harm in a walk, provided he knew exactly where she stood. She felt pressed to decide. Class was starting soon.

Hurriedly, she relented. "I'll walk with you after class if you'll meet me back here."

He grinned, relieved to hear it.

"But you better not try any of that handsy stuff," she added quickly. "I've got three brothers, and they taught me how to fight." Mama balled up her free hand, the one not carrying her books, and wiggled it at Daddy's nose.

"I'm not looking to get married, either. I already raised enough babies back home," Mama remarked before ducking inside.

Impressed by her fearlessness, Daddy whistled all the way to Hermeneutics. He was smitten but cautious. He knew there were as many Biblical admonitions against foolishness in general as there were songs about fools in love.

Daddy wasn't sure which category he'd fallen into. He knew he had been singed by Mama's titian ferocity, but he also had a hunch he might hand her a whole pack of matches if she wanted them. He dabbed his sweaty forehead with a handkerchief, suspecting all would be revealed after their walk.

Daddy decided he would ask Mama out for a fountain drink if their stroll went well. Daddy was a gentleman, but after Mama's impassioned castigation and the heat of the morning, it seemed prudent to be in the vicinity of cold beverages. That way, all bases would be covered in case he felt the need to dunk his head in a bucket of ice or she felt the need to practice her right hook.

THE FIRST FAMILY
OF SCRUFFY CITY

Knoxville, Tennessee, was not so special. It's true we were located at the base of the breathtakingly beautiful Smoky Mountains, but we didn't win any awards for culture or even cleanliness. Some visitors viewed our city as merely a convenient gas stop on their way to Silver Dollar City or Cades Cove. Others thought the place doubled as a garbage dump, judging by the amount of discarded Styrofoam cups and cigarette butts along the highway.

The average Knoxvillian, independent to a fault and about as fancy as a fishing trophy, didn't care much about what visitors thought either way.

Just how on Earth Knoxville ended up hosting the 1982 World's Fair remains one of the decade's greatest mysteries. Everyone was surprised. A big city journalist wrote about us, horrified that an ugly little town like Knoxville would even try to associate itself with grander sites of former World's Fairs like New York City or Paris. Overcome with disdain but only telling the truth, he called Knoxville a "scruffy little city" in his article.

Knoxvillians' pride was stung. How dare some walleyed cosmopolitan sit in judgment of our city from his Manhattan high rise! Most Knoxvillians did not find the smell of a damp Bronx subway car exquisite or enjoy the cozy feeling of a gun barrel pressed tightly against them during a routine mugging, like the journalist apparently did.

Despite a lack of avant-garde theatre troupes or rat-viewing opportunities, Knoxville was clearly a fine place to host a World's Fair, even accounting for scruffiness.

The city went to work and started building. The fair site was visible from Mama's favorite department store, Miller's, so Mama and I often stopped and watched the construction on our bus trips downtown.

The most exciting addition was the Sunsphere, a 266-ft steel column topped with a round observation deck. The Sunsphere frightened me. It looked like a colossal microphone, like what a scary giant might use if he were in a band.

I tried not to dwell too much on this fact. I did not want to think about my favorite singers, The Mandrell Sisters, growing nightmarishly big and using the Sunsphere to belt out one of their hits. If Barbara grew tall enough to pluck it from its large metal base, how big would that make her hair? Would her stylish blonde poof even fit in the sky? And what if Irlene dropped one of her gigantic drumsticks? We'd all be killed!

By the time the fair opened, I had developed a phobia of the Sunsphere. I also had a new baby sister.

In the early '70s, Daddy returned to work at the same radio station he had left to go to seminary. He ran out of tuition money after his first year and came back home to Tennessee. At least he won Mama as a consolation prize. Despite Mama's fierce protestations of matrimony, she and Daddy tied the knot after a brief courtship. I was born in the middle of their sixth year of marriage, during Daddy's stint as an associate pastor at a local Baptist church.

Mama had taken a chance on Daddy, thinking that serving time as a pastor's wife might further her own goals of working in children's ministry. It turned out that both were ill-suited for such formalities.

Daddy was conflicted. While he appreciated the church's approach to tradition and respect, he viewed its formality as a hindrance to truly worshiping the Lord. In his experience, the example of Jesus' humility and gentleness often took a backseat when a congregation emphasized attendance numbers or budgets instead of love and compassion.

And Mama, well, Mama had pretty much sealed her fate when she confronted that Jezebel at church.

"When your daddy first started preaching," she told me, "this one woman kept trying to pray with him by herself, away from everybody else. She was real pretty, but she was *sly*. She pretended like she was fainting from the presence of the Holy Spirit so your daddy could catch her. I didn't trust her, and your daddy is a babe in the woods and didn't understand what she was trying to do.

"So, I went over to her house. When she opened the door, I told her, 'You better leave my husband alone.'

"She said, 'I ain't doing nothing wrong. If I want to pray with him, I will.'

"'No, you won't,' I told her, and then I whooped her. I whooped her good."

Mama and I had a close relationship from the start. Perhaps too close. In retrospect, maybe telling this to a three-year-old was another sign that children's ministry, or any ministry, wasn't for her.

Daddy had gone from preaching in front of a congregation to preaching once a week on his mentor's radio program to not preaching formally at all. Instead, he used his time back in the DJ's booth to encourage and uplift the radio audience between songs. Daddy seemed happy with this decision, but it was no secret he didn't make much money. In fact, being paid in actual fishes and loaves would have been worth more than the peanuts he made at the radio station.

Mama still spent her time in service to children, namely Sissy and me, but she wasn't especially happy. She made that known a million different ways, and while it should never have been my burden, I longed to make her feel better. I know Daddy did, too.

One of the few perks of working at the station was access to free tickets to local events. That included the World's Fair. Once the tickets were in her hand, Mama decided to spend an entire day at the Fair with Sissy and me. Daddy made plans to meet us after work; this brief opportunity was his only chance to attend.

Mama and I hit the fairgrounds early one summer day. She pushed Sissy around in a colorful canvas stroller. Sissy, adorably smooshed into her seat and looking like a sweet potato wearing a sunhat, slept most of the morning. I could not. I was overwhelmed with delight by all I saw but purposely did not gaze upon the Sunsphere. It towered over me menacingly. When I glanced in its direction, the Sunsphere appeared to yaw dangerously to the right, ready to fall and be scooped up by a humongous version of Louise, the brunette Mandrell sister.

I decided to focus on the good things, like the pair of sparkly blue deely boppers Mama bought for me and the six-foot-tall, motorized ketchup bottle. Apparently, a ketchup bottle big enough to hug was a perfectly geared marketing campaign for a kid my age, considering how much of the stuff

I dumped on the French fries I had for lunch. After a long walk to and from the Ferris wheel – which I was also afraid of – and a short snooze bunched up against Mama's arm, it was almost time for Daddy to meet us.

We had time for one more activity.

"You want to go up in the Sunsphere?" Mama asked. Her tone wasn't gentle, exactly, but it was kind. Mama was as intrepid as they came. This was in stark contrast to me. Even at age three, I felt neuroses developing in my brain, as inevitable as yellow daffodils popping through the dirt each spring.

"I'm scared of it, Mama," I told her.

"Well, why don't we try?" she said. "We can always come down if you get too scared."

Trying my best to be brave, I plodded heavily toward the elevator at the bottom of the structure, keeping my eyes on my shoes so I wouldn't catch a glimpse of the top of the Sunsphere. I held Mama's hand firmly as we stepped into the elevator car along with a dozen other people.

When the doors opened, we were ushered onto the observation deck. At first, the backsides of our large group shielded me from seeing the enormous, curved windows designed to present an unencumbered 360-degree view. To my horror, however, the lights suddenly dimmed. A warbly soundtrack wound up to speed and began describing the construction of the Sunsphere.

I quickly realized another fear I had about the Sunsphere – *being in the dark while inside the Sunsphere.* I gripped Mama around her waist and closed my eyes, remembering every scary monster I had ever seen – a cartoon devil, a Halloween ghost, Bruce Banner's piercing green eyes when he turned into the Hulk on TV. I was literally in the belly of the beast, or more accurately, its mouth. I was terrified.

The soundtrack ended quickly, and the lights were restored to my immense relief. I opened my eyes slowly. The backsides were still there. I touched the deely boppers on my head, also still intact.

I was thrilled I had survived. I shouted exuberantly, "That was so scary, Mama! I thought the Hulk was going to get me, but he didn't!"

"You did good, Heather Pooh," Mama smiled.

The crowd dispersed throughout the circular observation deck, and the view of Knoxville was finally revealed. Gingerly, I approached the railing, which was taller than I was. The advancing dusk had softened the contrast of the sky from the ground, further deflating my fear. The lights of downtown Knoxville began to glow. I watched in wonder.

After a few minutes, Mama took my hand, and we rode the elevator back down to the fairgrounds. We met Daddy right after. I ran to him excitedly. He scooped me into his arms and carried me while I chattered on about my day.

Daddy didn't make it in time to see much before the Fair closed for the day, but we stopped to watch the nightly fireworks display on our way to the bus stop. Safely ensconced in Daddy's arms, I bravely looked in the direction of the Sunsphere. A different part of the city was reflecting itself in each gold panel. Every twinkle seemed like a friendly wink meant just for me. I wasn't afraid anymore.

I sat beside Daddy on the bus. I held one of his hands while Mama sat on the other side, adjusting Sissy in her stroller. Once Sissy was sleeping peacefully, Mama sunk back in her seat. After a long moment, she folded Daddy's other hand into hers.

Grownups were still largely a mystery to me, but I could tell our family had a good day, even Mama. I was worn out and hot but happy.

The bus dipped into a pothole, wiggling the springs of my deely boppers. I bobbed my head back and forth to make them move faster. Tilting my head toward the fairgrounds, I wiggled goodnight to the Sunsphere as we crossed the bridge before it dropped out of sight.

PROJECT MANAGER

I know most people wouldn't be thrilled to move back to the projects, but I was. After spending an entire year sleeping on Mammaw's bedroom floor, I was ready for a twin bed of my own and the freedom to spend more than ninety interrupted seconds in the bathroom.

Before Mammaw's house, we had lived in a housing project in Harriman, TN. Harriman was a tiny town founded on temperance and nestled along a ridge near the Emory River. It was an idyllic little place with a downtown diner and a small, cozy library.

I lived in paradise. My kindergarten teacher, a regional Teacher of the Year winner, was of the finest caliber of educators, and I adored her. Our church, the big Baptist one in the historic district, served only the good cookies during Sunday school (chocolate chunk and pecan sandies), never the generic oatmeal ones with the rough, burned edges that would scratch your tongue. Even the laundromat was superior. It smelled more like detergent than cigarettes, unlike everything else in Tennessee during the '80s.

The housing project in Harriman was not bad at all. Kids were free-range but never out of sight of *somebody's* mama. I might have played outside wearing only my Wonder Woman-branded Underoos, but it was understood I was imitating my favorite superhero and not because I had no-good parents who let me wander out of the house without pants. My tricycle, perpetually left in the yard, remained unmolested and on our property.

In general, the neighborhood kids were a respectable bunch. No one needed the humiliation of hearing a gravelly-voiced chain-smoking mother, perched froglike on the front stoop, yell at us while her gigantic braless bosom jiggled with emotion against her thighs.

Brawling, panhandling, and starry-eyed busking also seemed far away, as befitting a town with no liquor store.

Daddy had followed his radio gig from Knoxville to a different station in Harriman. Same owner, same autonomy, same Christian music, same piddling paycheck. By the end of the school year, the Harriman station wasn't doing well. Mom wasn't happy, either, living in a small, sleepy town that reminded her too much of the one in which she had been raised. My parents began to talk about moving back to Knoxville.

Although I missed my extended family, I liked Harriman. I had friends at school and in our neighborhood. I had earned a Good Citizen award at my school, and my picture made it into the local paper. Once, a neighbor even gave me an entire pack of gum because I helped load her car with stuff for her flea market booth. I was living like a tiny queen.

Even Sissy, the world's most fearless toddler, seemed to be thriving. Things were great despite her ending up with stitches after jumping off the bed and cracking her head on the linoleum floor. She was well on her way to future glory, interested in learning my kindergarten vocabulary words as well as attempting to set a world record for Most Consecutive Bowls of Froot Loops Eaten.

The Harriman station folded. Daddy was invited back to work at the Knoxville station, so we went. We were put on a waiting list for public housing and had no place to go in the meantime except Mammaw's. I wasn't looking forward to living in someone else's house, but I didn't have much say in the matter.

If only I had been able to work in the hosiery mill and pull in some decent money, like the croupy, exploited, Suntanned Appalachian children of the past, maybe we could have stayed. If only!

Back in Knoxville, we were welcomed into my grand-mother's house. She gave up her room so Mama and Daddy could sleep in her bed. Sissy and I slept beside Mama and Daddy on the floor, sharing a twin mattress. Every morning, we would stand the twin mattress up against the side of the big bed, allowing Mammaw to access her dresser and closet before going to work.

For twelve months - *long* months - Mammaw slept on the couch. Two of my uncles, the youngest of her seven children, lived in the other two bedrooms.

We all shared a tiny bathroom, the same bar of soap, and the same bottle of shampoo. Remarkably, no one had to pee at the same time someone else was washing their hair, unless, of course, the person peeing and washing hair was the same. (I, for one, tried not to ruminate on this efficiency and had no other comment on the matter.) However, that meant you were either waiting on someone to finish up in there or trying not to take too long yourself. This was hardly a relaxing situation, especially for a six-year-old who couldn't reach the lock to ensure privacy.

On the other hand, meals were delicious and mostly prepared by Mammaw. Because she trusted no one in her family to prepare even the simplest of dishes, Mammaw had been cooking for fifty years without a break. It was weird watching her stir gravy in her dreams.

Although Mammaw was Tennessee's most territorial chef, her culinary ability allowed her to easily accommodate four more people, despite what else she had going on in her life. Even so, I'm convinced she often fantasized about stocking the freezer with TV dinners and leaving us to fend for ourselves just so she could put on her house shoes and go watch the evening news for once.

I understood how she felt. When I needed a break from everybody, I would sit quietly under the dining room table and eat toothpaste directly from the tube. Every burst of cinnamon was a happy and potentially toxic reminder that at least I was eating something Mammaw didn't have to prepare.

Fresh breath, too.

Somehow, we survived. We were welcomed into my grandmother's home, but as soon as a public housing apartment became available, she was glad to see us go.

～

WESTERN HEIGHTS WAS THE name of the new housing project. At first, I loved our new place, a two-story duplex with a generous yard. The Baptist Center, one of the onsite charities, furnished our living room and kitchen. We had a couple of scratchy armchairs that gave you rugburn on the backs of your thighs if you happened to slide forward too quickly and a round wooden table that held our small TV. Unfortunately, there wasn't enough seating for all four of us unless someone dragged a chair from the kitchen into the living room.

That didn't matter much to me since Daddy worked so

much, and Mama was always on her feet, but she still took offense. Although Mama had belonged to a Baptist church for years, she felt that many of the brethren were snooty and completely unprepared for her big personality and loose interpretations of Christian doctrine.

"Didn't them heifers have a couch they could give us? Jesus wouldn't want us to watch *Highway to Heaven* sittin' on the floor!" Mama would grumble, conveniently forgetting our Savior's humble beginnings.

We shared the duplex with a single mom, her deaf eight-year-old son, Billy, and her infant daughter. The lady was nice enough but didn't remind me of the free-range mamas of Harriman. She seemed too eager to please and a little desperate. Billy's father wasn't in the picture, but her daughter's father still came to visit. Our neighbor confided in my mom, who, as usual, confided in me that Billy had behavior problems.

We had only been there a few days, but Mom and I had already watched a few of Billy's outbursts outside our front window. He would sign lightning fast to his mother, a furious expression on his face, and then storm back into the apartment. Their language fascinated me, but I was afraid to get too close. There was anger in Billy's eyes that was unspoken but seemed understandable. Being a deaf kid in a hearing world seemed hard enough, but not having your daddy around to help you figure things out was awful. My heart felt like stone in my chest just thinking about it.

I began to settle into my new school and new routine. I met some of the other kids in our neighborhood. I tried to be friendly, but it was obvious we were on different wavelengths. One of the kids, a first grader, used the "f" word regularly while his friend, our neighbor on the opposite side, invited me to eat cat food.

"I think it's good," he told me one morning, crunched-up kibble obscuring his silver-capped smile. His cat meowed in agreement. "Want some?" he asked, offering up a handful in his moist palm. "No thanks," I said automatically. "Mom made pancakes."

Western Heights wasn't like the projects in Harriman. The kids were still free-range, but there was a dearth of Porch Mamas to keep them in check. Some of the kids were mean; all of them were neglected.

A group of three kids often played together on our block, a boy my age and a younger brother and sister from a different family. All of them were towheaded but so covered with actual dirt it turned their hair dark. They were sweet kids but clearly needed help.

Worse still, the boy my age, Walnut, seemed to like me a whole lot. He spent most of his time away from school jubilantly playing outside, wearing cut-off shorts and ragged flip-flops. If he saw me, he'd ask if I wanted to play with him. Sometimes, to be nice, I'd say yes.

One day, Sissy and I walked past Walnut, who was sitting in the street playing with his action figures. His legs were sprawled out in front of him, shoes askew. Our eyes followed the movement of his toys and fell on the crotch of Walnut's shorts, which had a sizeable hole in them. There was no underwear in sight.

"Hi, Walnut. Bye, Walnut," we greeted him as we hurried inside.

I went straight to Mama. "Mom, Walnut is sitting outside, and he doesn't have any underwear on, and he's just *sitting* there!" I said breathlessly.

Mama leapt up from the chair and pulled back the curtain. I'm not sure what she expected to see, but she relaxed when she saw Walnut wearing clothes. Mom looked at me, eyebrow raised. I explained the situation in more detail.

"Good Lord, honey!" Mama said sharply. "He probably don't have no underwear, that's why."

I felt bad I hadn't considered it, but didn't Walnut live in the projects, same as us? We were poor, too, but I knew my mother would bargain her soul for an enchanted loom before she let any of us be *that* breezy and unrestrained.

"He might not have any underwear, but he doesn't have to let it all hang out!" I retorted proudly.

Mom said nothing, but I sensed agreement in her silence. She paused before closing the curtain, her gaze fixed on the two other children gathered with Walnut. The young brother shared Walnut's toys. The action figures did not interest the young girl, who instead happily struck the pavement over and over with a large rock.

"Lord, those kids are filthy," Mama muttered, "They ain't takin' good care of them babies."

Suddenly, Mama opened the door and went out into the street. Walnut saw her coming and grabbed his toys to leave. In his world, no parent moved that quickly unless they were mad. The siblings, Walnut's abandoned casualties, were still processing his swift retreat when Mama's hands encircled theirs.

"Come on inside, kids," she said, "y'all need a bath."

They obeyed wordlessly, and I watched all three of them climb the stairs and walk into the bathroom. Before Mom shut the door, she called down to us on the first floor. "Girls! Find some clean clothes for them."

Sissy and I rushed upstairs to our room. Both kids were approximately Sissy's size, which meant both kids were going home in her clothes. Sissy knew there was no guarantee she would get her clothes back. She skipped over her favorites and selected items she wouldn't miss.

From the bathroom, we heard splashing and Mama doing funny voices.

"Oh, oh! We're gonna wash that hair real good," she said, imitating the agitator in the center of a washing machine. "Reet-reet-reet-reet." The kids seemed to be having a pretty good time.

Knowing how strongly Mama felt about underwear, Sissy and I also picked out two older pairs that would fit both the brother and the sister. I knocked on the bathroom door and handed Mom the clothes. Mom gathered their dirty clothes in a bag when the kids were dressed and walked them outside.

"Tell your mama I was the one who gave y'all a bath if she asks," she said kindly but efficiently, handing the bag to the little boy. In a show of dominance, Mom did not walk the kids home to explain the situation in person. It was a bold move that would force unhappy parents to travel to her and dispense any outrage on her turf.

Mom wasn't exactly sure who their mother was, and she didn't care. If the mother didn't want neighbors bathing her kids, she should have taken better care of them in the first place. Mama was as close to the adults at Western Heights as I was to the children. She had met a lot of hotheads there and understood the importance of the home-court advantage.

We all said bye to each other, and the kids left. Mom returned upstairs and started scrubbing out the tub, which was now ringed with dirt. She had solved a problem and felt satisfied. Righteous in her decision, she had but one comment.

"I hate I had to send that little boy home in flowered underdrawers."

I replied, "He's still better off than Walnut."

Mama never heard from the kids' mother, but she never had to bathe them again, either. We continued to be polite but detached from surrounding neighbors as the months passed. People always seemed on the verge of getting into fights, especially the women.

It wasn't uncommon for a skirmish, verbal or otherwise, to erupt while waiting in line for commodities. Every month, each household was given powdered milk, peanut butter, and other basics to stretch our food budgets. Cutting the line was forbidden, but it was near impossible for some folks not to try.

I suppose it was eager anticipation for delicious government cheese that agitated so many, or perhaps just the daily crushing reminder of poverty and anxiety of the future. After all, if you don't have access to a great education or a way to build generational wealth, a slab of tangy, perfectly soft cheese lying atop a federal-brand cracker was surely a decent consolation prize.

With these things in mind, Mom and Daddy started trying to scrape together enough money to move. They were not mollified in the slightest by a dairy product disguised as Uncle Sam's manna, nor did they intend to get into a fistfight waiting for a bag of pinto beans.

I continued to play after school with two little girls who lived nearby. They thought I was a goody-two-shoes. I guess I was if being a goody-two-shoes meant staying out of trouble and knowing how to count to ten without having to take off my shoes and socks. Sadly, I had also witnessed their casual cruelty to siblings and other kids. They weren't happy unless they were excluding someone or making fun of them.

It seemed best to play with them occasionally in hopes of focusing their torment away from me. Being a disapproving member of their club was safer than never hanging out with them at all and, therefore, not knowing what they were planning, at least until the afternoon they started in on Billy.

That day after school, Billy halfheartedly waved hi before going inside his apartment. He usually avoided us, with good reason.

"He's retarded!" said the older and mouthier girl, mocking Billy's guttural speech. The younger girl laughed.

"He's not retarded!" I shouted back at her. "He can't hear. That's just how his voice sounds!" I was livid. Why did she have to be so mean?

The older girl and I stared at each other, her flinty blue eyes searching mine for any weakness. I've since imagined it was the same look she gave her inevitable cellmate the first time they met.

My gaze gave no quarter. We were locked in a power struggle, silently clashing. The younger girl, eager for a winner to worship, waited expectantly. A fly could have landed in her mouth, so slack-jawed was she from excitement.

Finally, the older girl began to sing, "Heather loves Billy! Heather loves a retard!"

"I don't love Billy!" I yelled. "But who cares if I did!"

I stormed off into our apartment, slamming the screen door behind me. *Dookieheads!* I thought. Their stupidity was infuriating.

A few days later, the girls showed up again.

"We're really sorry," said the older one contritely. "We won't make fun of Billy again. Can we still be friends?"

Still sore over the way they treated him but remembering what I had learned in Sunday School about forgiveness, I said yes. I was relieved to put the conflict behind us.

The older one continued, "We wanted to show you a new game. It's *Apple on a Stick*, but you close your eyes when you clap to see how fast you can go."

Apple on a Stick was one of the half-dozen hand-clapping games elementary school girls knew. They were a lot of fun to practice, especially if you could recite the rhyme quickly and accurately. Perfecting a game with closed eyes sounded like a cool challenge.

I followed them outside and sat down in the yard across

from the older girl. The younger girl stayed off to the side. I closed my eyes and started clapping.

"Apple on a stick, makes me sick. Makes my heart go two-forty-six."

Suddenly, the older girl leaned forward. She grabbed hold of my mane and pulled hard. I felt a flash of pain. I opened my eyes and saw the older one on her feet, holding a chunk of my hair. She dropped it thoughtlessly, like a vicious dog dropping a dead bird and ran back across the street with the younger girl. I was speechless, stunned by their cowardly plot. In the next second, my scalp started to throb. I reached up and felt the quarter-sized bald spot where my hair used to be.

I inhaled deeply, breath hitching over my tears. With all my might, I shrieked one word, "Mamaaaaaaaaaaa!"

Mama ran out of the apartment and over to me.

"Heather Pooh, what's wrong?" she screeched.

"A girl pulled my hair, Mama," I cried, "They tricked me and pulled my hair out. It hurts!"

Mama gasped when she saw the bald spot on top of my head.

"Where did they go?"

"Back to the girl's house across the street," I wailed.

"Come on. We're gonna go over there and show her mother what her little brat did."

"No, Mama, I don't want to see that girl anymore," I said.

"You won't. She's gonna be too scared to come outside after this."

After what, I wondered worriedly. Reluctantly, I crossed the street with Mama but held back, standing in the girl's yard while Mama banged on the door. A woman opened it. She had dirty blonde hair and the same stony blue eyes as my assailant.

Mom had no time for pleasantries. "Look what your daughter did to my little girl's hair! She ripped it right out!"

Mama pushed me closer to their porch. I bent my head so the woman could see it. She looked without comment and called her daughter's name. The older girl appeared in the doorway. The younger girl was nowhere to be seen.

"Did you pull her hair?" the woman asked.

"Yes, but we were playing," the girl said, lying bold as brass. "I didn't mean to."

"You liar!" I screamed, tears falling once more. "You said you wanted to be my friend again and told me to close my eyes, and then you pulled my hair!" I was seething from humiliation and hurt.

The woman seemed unmoved. "You should say you're sorry," she said to her daughter. Her offer of a resolution was not magnanimous; it was one of disengaged routine. Either she thought we were making too much of a fuss about things, or she was used to initiating amends for the girl.

Sullenly, the girl said, "Sorry," and ducked back into their apartment.

Mama was not satisfied. Before she left their porch, she made herself clear.

"You keep your kid away from my little girl, you hear? If anything like this happens again, I'll whoop both of y'all."

The girl's mother finally reacted, anger lighting up her face like a plane full of napalm dropped in the dark of night.

"Don't talk to me like that, you piece of trash!" the woman yelled. "We'll do what the hell we want. You can kiss my ass!"

Alarmed by how quickly the situation had escalated, I scurried back to our side of the street. My mother, having begun her own walk home, stopped in the middle of the road. She posed purposely as if on stage in front of a large audience. Playfully wiggling her own *derriere*, she called back over her shoulder to the woman, "Stick it up here, baby, and we'll call it a love story."

Flabbergasted, the woman closed the door. And locked it.

A few weeks later, Mama and Daddy shared some wonderful news. They had found an inexpensive house to rent on the south side of town, near Mammaw's. Our future place sat next door to the landlady's house and two doors down from a large Baptist church. After the last year, we were all looking forward to a fresh start. I had learned the hard way that not all housing projects were the same.

Since the end of the school year was close, it seemed wisest to stay away from all the kids, whether they liked me or not. I no longer had to worry about trying to fit in with the cat-food eaters and depilators. That seemed to be Mama's plan, too. Mentally, she had started to pull up stakes; there wasn't any point in pretending she'd miss the neighbors.

It was late in the evening when we heard a ruckus outside. Mom, Sissy, and I had been watching TV in the living room after a long day of packing. Hearing loud male voices, Mom got up from her scratchy armchair and stealthily peeked out the curtain.

I whispered, "Mama! What's going on?"

"Hush, Heather. I can't hear them," she whispered back.

Daddy was still at work, leaving Mama alone to protect her brood from whatever antics were taking place outside. She paused, weighing the probability of danger – or perhaps another exasperated rebuke from my father - against her own curiosity, and slowly opened the door a few inches.

Two men were on our porch, talking to Billy's mom. One of them I recognized as her baby's father, who sometimes stayed at their apartment. Furthermore, I knew what beer smelled like from sniffing empty Bud cans left on Mammaw's kitchen table. Beer smell radiated from these two men as if they had fallen into a lake of it.

With Mama blocking the door, I still couldn't make out

what they were saying; however, they sounded raucous and irritable. I heard Billy's mom try to talk over them, but she was drowned out by the men's volume and the river of alcohol they had imbibed.

Sensing trouble, Mama opened the security door fully and stood watch behind the screen.

"Let me in, you bitch!" the baby's father yelled, "That's my daughter! I want to see my daughter!"

Billy's mom sounded frightened but didn't waiver. "No! You're drunk. You ain't gonna see her if you're drunk. Y'all get out of here!"

"I'll see her any damn time I want!" he replied, staying put on the porch while his friend steadied himself against an iron post.

Inside our apartment, Mama bristled. She had had enough of hearing these hooligans harass her neighbor, of witnessing other parents visit their bad choices upon innocent children, of Western Heights in general. It was time to put a stop to this nonsense.

Impulsively, she grabbed the only weapon within reach, her fat, hand-annotated Bible.

"You and Sissy stay inside this house," she commanded.

Mama flung open the screen door, clutching the heavy Bible in her right hand. She thrust it out in front of her, the porchlight accentuating the imitation leather cover featuring her name embossed in gold.

"*I rebuke you, Satan, in the name of Jesus!*" she yelled mightily. "Now, get off this porch and *go home!*"

The men were astonished by Mama's rambunctious admonition. Speechless, they couldn't even manage to laugh.

The beer wasn't the only spirit present that night. Mama continued to pray out loud, rebuking the men and asking the Lord to cover the duplex with a hedge of protection.

"Everybody thinks I'm nuts, heavenly Father," she said, in passive-aggressive supplication to the Lord. "And maybe I am, but these men are gonna get their sorry asses thrown in jail if they don't get out of here right now!"

Recognizing she meant business, the two men quickly lumbered away from the porch and headed towards a beat-up car.

"Let's get out of here," said one of them nervously. "She's crazy!"

They left, tires squealing. Mom watched them drive away. Though she had walked through the valley of shenanigans, Mama feared no fools. After comforting Billy's mom, she came back inside.

The excitement was over. She lay her Bible on the armchair along with her pack of cigarettes, ready for her devotion time the next morning. Still coursing with adrenaline but convinced God was on Mom's side in all matters of justice, I plopped down on the floor and went back to watching TV.

On our last day, we filled Mammaw's Cadillac with our belongings. We said brief goodbyes to a few neighbors, including Billy and his mom. I waved bye to him, feeling sad but not understanding why. I squeezed into the backseat of the car, pressed into a stack of boxes. I had no choice but to sit rigidly, facing forward as we pulled away from the duplex.

I wondered what I would see if I could turn around and watch the projects recede in the distance. Probably Walnut, who would be sitting in the middle of the road as usual, airing his grievances. But maybe Billy as well, standing behind his screen door and waving back at me.

From the other side of the boxes, Mom spoke. "Lordy, Lordy. Ain't this Skid Row for sure." It was not a question but a declaration. It had been our home.

"Bless 'em, Lord," she added in benediction.

PLAYING TAG

*C*uriosity. Creativity. Anxiety. They were my constant companions in childhood. Naturally, my educators determined that I needed a series of evaluations and inquiries to root out the problem. Meetings were held, and I was quizzed thoroughly.

In fact, I can report I was the inaugural student at Beaumont Elementary to take a Rorschach test in the cafeteria. The menu that day was watery chili and mushy peanut butter sandwiches, a repast well-suited for incredulous speculation of all kinds, including recipe ingredients. After careful consideration by school psychologists, I was given a diagnosis.

I tested positive for "giftedness."

I owed it all to Mama. The four of us - Mama, Daddy, Sissy, and I – had just moved to Western Heights, a Knoxville housing project. Our arrival there had been preceded by a year of sleeping on my grandmother's floor and sandwiched by a year of living in a different housing project.

My father worked full-time at a local Christian radio station that offered autonomy and a lack of micro-management in exchange for solo DJ duty, sunup to sundown, six days a week. Daddy was a bright and sensitive soul who loved ministering to his small radio audience, but after two housing projects in three years, probably even Jesus would have hung up his carpentry tools and applied for a different job at that point. Daddy didn't.

I had done well in first grade and enjoyed it immensely. During filmstrip time, my teacher let me help her grade papers while my classmates enjoyed tinny cassette soundtracks about phonics and learning to subtract from ten. Even more impressive, my good behavior earned me multiple prizes from the classroom treasure chest that year, putting me in the 99th percentile of keeping my hands to myself and focusing on my own work. Clearly, I was poised for continued success.

Now I was in a new school and a new grade and Mom was keen to make sure my teachers knew I was bright and had potential. On my first day of second grade, Mama asked about accelerated learning at the school. None was available. She then had a talk with the principal and asked if there was a 'talented and gifted' group I could be tested for instead. The principal told her no.

"You see, ma'am, we've never had a gifted program here at Beaumont. Our test scores don't support it," he said firmly. As an afterthought, he added, "With most of our students coming from Western Heights, we simply don't have a need for it."

Mama was furious. She remembered a stinging pronouncement from her own school days. A guidance counselor had once frostily discouraged Mom's dreams of higher education, telling her she "wasn't college material." This memory was burned into her forever.

At that moment, my principal became every stuck-up city-dweller who had ever hastily misjudged, whose cruelty had ever crumbled a carefully built house of hope, who had ever told Mama *no*.

"What about Heather?" she asked angrily. "She goes to Beaumont, and I know she's gifted!"

Trying to defuse the situation, he said, "If you really want her to be tested, you're going to have to speak to the superintendent's office."

So that's just what Mom did. She caught the city bus the day of her appointment, dragged my four-year-old sister with her, and talked to the superintendent directly. According to family lore, Mama unleashed such a passionate and vigorous imploration of my capabilities, plus the option of a knuckle sandwich, that he relented on the spot. He also allowed

Beaumont to identify and test other kids to create a talented and gifted program for the whole school.

It's also possible that the superintendent, a popular and well-respected educator, was moved by her plea and simply decided to do the right thing by his students even without the threat of bodily injury. Luckily for me, not everyone was a Goliath. Even so, Mama went everywhere with rocks in her pockets, just in case. She had learned the hard way that giants were plentiful.

After testing, a handful of students and I found ourselves the pioneers of Beaumont's TAG program. Once a week, I got to leave class and work independently in a small room attached to the office. It was perfect; I was left alone to work on ditto sheets and read. I could totally be myself, and what I wanted to be was alone. Alone to think, alone to sniff the intoxicating scent of the purple ditto ink deeply and repeatedly, alone to enjoy the quiet business of adults working around me.

Returning to my noisy classroom after this halcyon hour was such a bummer. I often walked back to class the long way, stopping to use the bathroom and slowly wash my hands. Bracing myself before the door, I knew that the world just wasn't set up for sensitive kids like me. Unfortunately, I still had to learn how to navigate it. At least a series of tests and my mom's bulldog assurance proved I was smart enough to understand this concept.

Looking on the bright side, the whole experience provided an early lesson in tolerance. No matter how much others intervened for my benefit or how hard I tried to craft and customize a happy environment, I inevitably found myself back in the classroom, outnumbered, once again seated next to a booger eater.

~

AT THE END OF second grade, we moved away from the projects for good. Miraculously, my parents found an affordable house to rent, and I was re-enrolled at my previous elementary school. I began their TAG program. I liked the facilitator and the other kids in the program, but I was overwhelmed from the start.

The TAG assignments in third grade became project-focused instead of writing-focused. Not only was I bereft of all artistic talent, but I was seriously worried we wouldn't have the money for needed supplies.

My fears were realized after our Egyptology project. Our assignment was to create a typical building that might have been a part of Cairo's landscape thousands of years ago. Daddy had helped me turn a shoebox and construction paper – the only art supplies in the house besides crayons and colored pencils – into a modest ancient home. It turned out better than expected, but I was unprepared for how good the other kids' projects were.

The most impressive was a large replica of the Great Pyramid made from modeling clay with tiny palm trees and priestly paraphernalia glued to its base. My confidence took a hit. I never even considered using any items but the ones we already had at home. I knew we couldn't afford to buy anything else, so I didn't even ask. I saw Daddy's pay stubs every week – they weren't hidden – and I knew what bills needed to be paid.

I considered the rest of the year. There would be more projects and field trips that were supposed to inspire a love of learning, but they would only teach me lack. I could never enjoy designing or creating anything I knew was literally taking food out of our mouths.

Nothing I could do could change the fact that my family was just as underfunded as the public school I attended.

Responsibility weighed heavy on me. That night, I spoke to my parents. I told them I didn't think my work was as good as the other kids', and I didn't want to be part of TAG any longer. Out of the deepest love for my daddy, I kept my thoughts about our poverty inside. Mama tried to persuade me to stay, but I told her no.

Mom wrote a long letter to my educational team with wide-ruled paper torn from my school notebook. In it, she said the program's extra work was creating too much anxiety for me. I was sensitive and had perfectionist tendencies, and if I couldn't do something accurately the first time, it was difficult for me to do it at all.

It was a smart letter because Mom was smart. After all, she had proven her snotty guidance counselor wrong and earned a degree in early childhood education. But it was also kind of dumb. All she really had to do was grab a broken crayon and write, "WE'RE TOO POOR FOR HER TO BE *THIS* SMART." They would have understood.

~2

BY EIGHTH GRADE, MORE money was flowing into the household. Now heavy with pocket change, my sister and I merely qualified for the *reduced* lunch fee at school instead of the free one. This meant we could afford the occasional pizza delivery or 99-cent video rental for our VCR, which was purchased in installments.

I joined the TAG program at yet another new school. Our TAG teacher was a young woman with long magenta hair and blunt bangs. She often wore a black turtleneck layered with several silver necklaces and matching rings. I thought she was cool and probably wore a beret everywhere outside the classroom, even to the grocery store. She assigned an awesome project, asking us to design a periodical based on ourselves. I was ecstatic.

I decided to imitate my favorite high-end fashion magazine. It was the era of the supermodel. Each of these otherworldly creatures was gorgeous with coltish legs, perfectly rendered faces, and 'tude to spare. Possessing all these qualities and more, I naturally chose my puffy-banged seventh-grade school picture as the cover shot.

Then, I lost myself in a creative frenzy. With our cheap family camera and roll of store-brand film, I decided to recreate every couture ad I had ever seen, with me as the star. Our trailer was too small and lacked necessary props, so I insisted Mom drive me to my grandmother's house for more inspiration. Once there, Mammaw allowed me to borrow her jewelry and pose all over the place. I got the feeling Mammaw didn't necessarily understand what I was doing, but she was quietly supportive. I tried to stay out of her way so she could watch *Designing Women* in peace.

I took pictures in almost every room. In the hallway, I inserted myself into a jewelry ad, my hand cradling my face, every finger fat with a different faux-stone ring. I dramatically clutched a recent bestseller in front of the fireplace, purporting to be the author. I used some of Mammaw's frosted lipstick and modeled for a perfume sitting at the dining room table.

These were all good ideas, but I needed more variety. The high-fashion magazine I was paying tribute to was primarily geared toward women, but every issue had an ad or two featuring men.

Luckily, my cousin Brayden happened to be around that

night. He and I were the same age, but where I might be the angel on your shoulder, he might be the devil. He was constantly getting into trouble but managed to charm his way out of any punishment. Practically every girl at his school had a crush on him, and he always got what he wanted for Christmas. I adored him, but I also knew better than to trust him completely.

He was the perfect bad boy for my cologne ad.

We created his character. The copy was, "This is Geoffrey. He's a model. He wears *X Brand* cologne." I then directed his styling. He slicked back his hair, and I drew a black eyeliner mustache on his fuzzy upper lip. Brayden sifted through an ashtray on a bedside table and picked up the remainder of a hand-rolled cigarette. He unbuttoned his shirt and peeled off his smelly socks to give Geoffrey a beach vibe. It was a usable look but needed more.

Also on the bedside table was a pistol. This was not an unusual occurrence. Mammaw had six grown sons, and every one of them, except my daddy, was an avid hunter or shooter. Mammaw's house was like Grand Central Station. She was never home alone. There was bound to be a gun or two lying around because some uncle was always taking off a holster, showing off a new purchase, or cleaning one.

The world was a different place then. Tennessee, its own planet.

No one ever got hurt, as far as I know. This was probably because if someone in my family was stupid enough to accidentally shoot someone or perhaps found themselves the hapless recipient of a buttock wound, my uncles would ridicule them so mercilessly that they might decide to die on purpose just to escape the judgment.

Brayden positioned himself on the twin bed, cigarette fragment in mouth, his hand gently gripping the pistol across his chest. His bare feet said "Maui," while the rest of him said "prodigy Bond henchman."

Geoffrey's look was complete: Guns-'N-Poses.

Later, I had my pictures developed and put all the pages together. I was proud of it. My cover story *Supermodel of the Decade* was unrealistically braggadocious and boasted that I, in addition to being the world's greatest supermodel and author, "had completed both high school and college in three years," which I guess made sense when you factored in all the imaginary cocaine. I turned in my assignment and awaited my grade.

At our next meeting, the teacher wanted to talk about my project. "Can you tell me more about this?" she asked, flipping the stiffly mucilaged pages over to Brayden's ad.

"Is that a cigarette in his hand?" Her tone was casual, but I could tell she was carefully modulating it. A hot flash tore through my body, and I suddenly understood she thought

Brayden was holding a joint. I wanted to crawl through the floor and disappear.

"Yes!" I shrieked. "My uncle thinks filters are for wimps. He hand-rolls all his cigarettes."

"And where did you get the gun?"

My mind was racing like a turbo-charged hamster wheel.

"It... it belongs to one of my uncles. We used it for the picture and then put it right back down. I swear."

I wondered if she had talked about me to her boyfriend over a turtle cappuccino the night before, their matching berets tilting in astonishment as they looked over my high-fashion evidence locker.

She didn't say anything for a minute, trying to figure out if I was a genius provocateur or just a stupid ass kid.

"Okay," she said finally. "I really liked your magazine."

I got an A, but I was tired of playing TAG. For the third and final time, I quit. I had narrowly escaped a sullied reputation, owing nothing to my intelligence. Fortune may favor the bold, and indeed I could have been considered bold, but this was only dumb luck.

1972

1982

FISKE HEIGHTS, HARRIMAN, TN

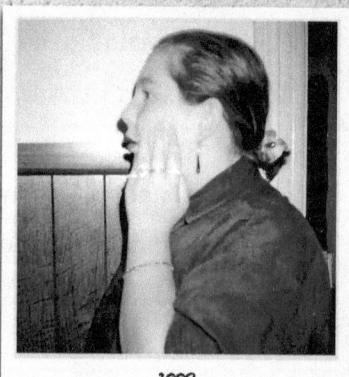

1992

THEY KNOW NOT WHAT THEY DO

I was six when I received my first lesson in Christian hypocrisy. Naturally, it occurred in the church sanctuary. It was the last day of Vacation Bible School, and a dozen of us kids were performing songs about God's creation. The reprise included a chorus of a famous gospel title track about creekbanks. This was our big finale, and we were instructed to hold hands and sway to the music.

I had spent the week at VBS mastering Bible verse memorization, crafting (just so we're clear, my peanut butter-and-birdseed-pinecone was a true work of art), and choreography. I thoroughly enjoyed myself, and our exuberant musical program was a fantastic way to end on a high note. I was proud that Mama, Daddy, Mammaw, and Uncle Mark were watching me from the audience. They laughed at the funny parts and clapped heartily after each song.

I was born to perform. At least, I thought I was until I reached for the hand of the girl standing beside me, as previously rehearsed. As soon as I touched her hand, she sharply pulled away from me. Hatefully.

It was as if time stood still. I was in shock that she would behave in such a manner. Why didn't she want to hold hands with me now? Did she not like me? Had I done something to hurt her feelings? We barely knew each other.

Wait. Was it cooties? I knew I didn't have cooties. That was just a ridiculous thing that kids said about other kids they wanted to be mean to. But why?

I stood, frozen. Li'l Hateful Helen clasped the hand of the kid on her left side with no problem, a simper plastered on her face as she swayed cutely. Even though actors are trained to handle the unexpected on stage – a forgotten line, a missed cue – I did not possess this skill. The show was expected to go on, right?

Yeah, right. Emotional from the heartbreak, I dramatically ran off the dais and into Mama and Daddy's arms, sobbing. Even more heartbreaking, the music continued, and the kids finished the song without me.

The lights came back on in the sanctuary as my family comforted and commiserated with me. They all saw what had happened and understood why my feelings were hurt.

I saw the girl with her family after the program had ended. Her parents, highly regarded members of the church, happily hugged her. They did not seem disappointed in her actions. Perhaps they didn't notice what had happened or were just blind to her brattiness.

Neither of my parents went to talk to hers. That surprised me. My mama, the easily inflamed type, was always ready for a fight. I wasn't sure why she hadn't laced up her boxing gloves yet.

Having been trained in childhood education, she likely considered the issue insignificant. One first grader making another first grader cry onstage probably didn't even warrant a bullet point in a textbook. That's showbiz, after all.

Once I realized no apology was forthcoming, I redoubled my weeping efforts and heaved forth great sobs. In fact, I'm not sure why I wasn't awarded a scholarship to a children's theatre class at that very moment. I could certainly emote.

But it was only because I didn't have the vocabulary to articulate the bigger disappointment; someone was mean to me *at church.* That someone also happened to have a mom who got to sing a lot of choir solos and a dad who was a deacon.

We had just spent an entire week learning about Jesus and love and how Jesus cursed a fig tree one time, which seemed crazy to me because Fig Newtons were delicious. If a kid was mean to me at church, where everybody was supposed to be nice to each other and love each other, she wouldn't hesitate to be mean to me in any place at any time.

I had been taught that mean people didn't go to church. Some kids from Troubled Families might have acted rowdily sometimes during Sunday School, but they would never cut others to the quick like my simpering stage partner did. That was saying something, too, especially since the teacher might find an actual knife in a rowdy kid's pockets.

My Sunday School teachers were always saying that those of us who loved Jesus were supposed to be the kindest in any given situation. Jesus loved everyone, and He helped poor people and sick people, and if we loved Jesus, we should do those things, too.

We were even supposed to love our enemies, and that included odious little girls. Even though I understood the irony, following this tenet was much easier in theory. It seemed heinously unfair to have to love and forgive someone who treated you badly.

However, since Christianity was supposed to be all about following Jesus' example, I sucked it up and tried my best to turn the other cheek, er - hand, whatever.

Despite forgiving the little girl, I was still worried. What if she acted mean to other kids? Would a grown-up do anything about it? And if I didn't want her to get away with it, would that make Jesus mad? Did vengeance cancel out forgiveness? Or was I confusing justice for vengeance? Trying to understand these concepts made my budding brain smoke.

I could never get a straight answer about God stuff from anyone but Daddy. He was the most patient person I knew, but he was always at work.

I returned to Sunday School, as usual, the following week. The hurt had faded, but I had learned a painful lesson: *a church can be full of jerks, and you can't always depend on grown-ups to do anything about it.*

~

I WAS ALSO TAUGHT, albeit unintentionally, that cultivating healthy patterns and reasonable boundaries wasn't a crucial part of spiritual health. The concept that a Christian could place one's hope in Jesus for a mental health miracle the same way one could pray for physical healing was a foreign one.

I had heard plenty of prayer requests for physical healing. Some were common to our conservative, semi-rural area, like, "Please pray for my friend, Tonya, as she has been stricken with hoof-and-mouth disease," or "Please keep my grandma in your prayers. She's having surgery for the broken hip she got from kicking Jehovah's Witnesses off her porch."

"Oh, and her court date is in September, so please pray for a Christian judge."

If there were any pleas for help or prayer requests about

serious topics like abuse, adultery, or alcoholism, they weren't made in a public forum. It's reasonable to assume that sensitive topics were discussed privately, but I'm not sure they were discussed much at all. Or if they were, appropriate help was only to be sought inside the church rather than in secular counseling.

Our region's religious beliefs were often crossbred with generations of dysfunction. For instance, the Biblical commandment to "Honor your father and mother" might be twisted to excuse heavy-handed corporal punishment or outright physical abuse of kids.

Since this mistreatment of children had been handed down from parent to child for decades, those cycles usually didn't get broken. Abusive parents were far more likely to justify their misuse of the Bible instead of seeking help to be more Christlike.

Put another way, they literally tried to beat the hell out of a kid. That never did anything but ensure their progeny bore the scars of trauma.

Another popular behavior supposedly modeled on Jesus was to "love the sinner and hate the sin." The same people who would swear - on a whole stack of Bibles, of course – that they had absolutely no problem with gay people would have absolutely no problem telling an ugly joke or using a homophobic slur.

In their minds, they only used these slurs to emphasize their own masculinity and distance themselves from the sinner they supposedly loved. Oddly enough, they had no problem loving every other kind of sinner, like their buddies who gambled or the friends who dumped their first wives for youthful secretaries.

But not every Christian I knew acted like this. The very best Christians in my life, Daddy especially, were forgiving and funny, kindhearted even in their imperfection. Cruelty masquerading as love didn't match what I had been taught about Jesus. I grew greatly discouraged by the appalling behavior of the brethren, especially from adults who should have known better.

By the time I was in fifth grade, constant coverage of Jimmy Swaggart and the Bakkers had practically burned melodramatic tearstains into our old cathode ray tube TV. The idea of pastors – especially rich ones – acting disgracefully was no longer shocking. In fact, I had come to expect it.

For every ten Christians I encountered, whether child or adult, only one of them exuded the kindness, compassion, and generosity we were supposed to be known for. And that hurt. Although Sissy and I were well-behaved during Sunday School and generally sweet, we experienced standoffishness from many in our big Baptist church.

I think it was because we were poor and because Mama

didn't fit the mold of a typical Baptist lady. We were needy, always, and since Daddy worked at the station on Sundays, Mom took us to church by herself. Most people lingering in the halls between Sunday School and worship service beelined to the sanctuary once we walked in.

Adults, I noticed, only wanted to help as long they could help minimally, without sacrifice, from a distance. Mama wasn't too proud to ask for help. In fact, she thought the church was obligated to help and Christians obligated to give.

Mama would gift anything we had freely, even impulsively, if a need arose. I once overheard an argument. Daddy was upset Mama put our last $10 into the offering plate.

She viewed it as a symbol of faith in God's provision.

He viewed it as our gas money for the week.

"The Lord will bless us for it, dammit!" she said, slapping her hand on her Bible for emphasis.

She certainly showed bold faith, but from a practical viewpoint, it stunk. Miraculously, a relative ended up coming to the rescue and giving us $20. In Mom's eyes, this was an answered prayer, and it buttressed her belief about trusting God. Not even the recently collapsed savings and loans industry ever delivered a 100% ROI.

Mama's belief was the reason she was audacious in asking for help. The Lord obviously rewarded bold giving, so it was only sensible that the church assist in any way possible.

They would be the ones getting back double; it was a win-win.

Yet, they were often reluctant. It was even worse when Mom expected me to have the same fearlessness.

"Heather, you tell the Awana teacher we can't afford to buy your uniform. Tell him we don't have no money for extras."

"Do I have to?" I pleaded, knowing that even if the church paid for the uniform, I'd eventually earn pins and patches for Bible memorization that would cost something, too. Thinking about having to solicit an adult to pay for cheap metal pins filled me with dread. Begging for awards I earned fair and square was even worse than having to shill those fundraiser candy bars at school every year.

"Can't I just quit Awanas?"

Sometimes, quitters were the real winners. "That's fine," said Mom. "I'm tired of listening to all those verses from First Corinthians, anyway."

One of the most humiliating lessons came one Wednesday evening. The church served supper before Bible Study, and those present gathered to eat in the fellowship hall. The church had an industrial kitchen and would typically prepare food for around 125 people on Wednesday nights.

Food wasn't free, after all, so there was a charge to eat. The charge was nominal – maybe $2.50 a plate – but it was still more expensive than a fast-food meal for us.

Mama often asked the person in charge of the cash box if we could eat even when we couldn't pay. We weren't going hungry at home, but we didn't always get our fill or the best nutrition.

A Wednesday night church supper with lasagna, salad, and sheet cake seemed downright decadent compared to a typical meal of fried potatoes and Mama's cornbread.

The sour-faced women who tended the cash box never had the authority to make that decision and would have to summon a deacon for permission. A pleasant mustachioed man would materialize, and Mama would pirouette for a $7.50 loan so her children could experience the earthly pleasures of name-brand salad dressing and a slice of heat-n-eat garlic bread.

Sometimes, she only asked for $5.00 and would make a bologna sandwich for herself when she got home.

Mama didn't always pay them back. To their credit, they never turned us away, but why church leadership thought it necessary for my mother to demean herself in any way to feed her children is hard to understand.

As I've aged, my theological opinions have matured, and my questions about the mysteries of God have only grown larger. I've wrestled with every element of Christianity, from the atonement to the book of Zechariah. I've concluded I'm still a spiritual infant.

However, I am certain of one thing.

Jesus would not have charged my mother to eat dinner in His house.

This evening, the summoned deacon was more stern than usual.

He said firmly to Mama, "We'll let you go through and get some dinner tonight, no charge. But you're going to have to pay next time. We can't keep doing this."

He was no pushover, by God. Part of his responsibility as a deacon was to help maintain the assets of the church. His attitude was reminiscent of a governor who hoarded budget surpluses 'for a rainy day' despite his constituents lacking health insurance or clean drinking water.

The church couldn't keep doing this, feeding hungry children and a mother who occasionally wanted more than a bologna sandwich for dinner.

"Yes, that's fine," said Mama with dignity.

Another part of the deacon's responsibility was to help shepherd the flock. Shepherding sometimes meant doling out tough love. Perhaps this family would benefit from the budgeting class the church offered.

"Okay, good," he replied, smiling warmly. "We expect everyone to pay their share. It's only fair."

He briefly acknowledged Sissy and me with a smile and went on his way. He didn't seem bothered that we were in earshot.

I thought about what I had witnessed as I moved through the line. I tried to scoop my food daintily, not taking too much, wanting to be worthy of their charity.

This was the nicest church we'd ever belonged to. Almost everyone here was far more visibly wealthy than us. Yet, I was supposed to believe that this 500-member worship extravaganza with a two-story attached gym, nice carpeting, and weekly TV program couldn't afford to give out a free lasagna or two.

I didn't buy it. Not even as a ten-year-old.

I had learned another painful lesson: *a church can be full of jerks, and sometimes grown-ups are the jerks.*

Stress churned in my stomach. I burped, tasting chocolate cake. I did not want to throw up my free meal.

Not possessing the emotional aptitude to cope with being excluded because of our poverty or the Biblical scholarship to refute their twisted gospel, I instead plotted revenge. My scheming was sinful, so I didn't ask Jesus for help. Still, I prayed He understood.

~

SINCE OUR HOUSE WAS two doors down from the church, Mama often let us wander over there by ourselves when the Family Life Center was open. The Family Life Center was swanky by any standard. The first floor contained a school-sized gymnasium, indoor racquetball courts, a dining area, and a plexiglass booth where one could request board games and athletic equipment. Upstairs was a walking track and several classrooms that connected to the church.

The idea was that kids and parents could partake in physical activity or Parcheesi in a wholesome environment. Nobody cursed, not even if a basketball player got elbowed in the face, or the preacher's wife got her safety goggles cracked because of an errant serve.

Nobody was sexy, either, because all the moms who took aerobics had huge '80s perms. It was hard to lust after a shapely bottom in a leotard when distracted by a hairdo resembling an electrocuted mop.

Surprisingly, there wasn't an admission charge or fee to rent a racquet. Seems like a real missed opportunity, considering the windfall the church made off Wednesday night supper.

Mom trusted us not to get hit by a car or kidnapped in the sixty seconds it took to walk there. And in general, she trusted us to behave.

One Saturday afternoon, Sissy and I sat with my best friend, Marcy, in a booth at the Family Life Center. We were halfheartedly playing a board game, bored in the way kids who are too young to drive get bored.

Marcy was a good kid – smart, opinionated, and not afraid to stand up for her buddies or anyone else who needed help.

We had become fast friends after showing up to school unintendingly wearing matching outfits from Kmart. I had picked the magenta blouse and stirrup pants combo, and she the yellow. The outfits were similar, yet different, like us, and they had spent far too long hanging out next to the Kmart Icee machine, also like us.

Even though she attended a different Baptist church, Marcy was also, sadly, familiar with Christian hypocrisy. My big feelings about it were never too much for her. She knew how I felt about my church and how I felt about being poor. I could always count on her encouragement. Sometimes, my ideas weren't worth encouraging.

Todd was the name of the man in charge of the Family Life Center that day. I didn't like him. He was involved in the youth ministry, old enough to be an adult but still immature enough to connect with the youngsters. Typical of the adults at church, he seemed to only connect with people who looked and acted the most like him.

Todd was into sports and high-fiving the athletic kids who played in the gym. I failed the presidential fitness test every year and never completed a pull-up. We had nothing in common except our religion. I felt completely invisible around him, like a rotund towel boy in a regional playoff locker room.

Wanting to switch out our board game, I approached the plexiglass booth. It was empty. Todd had disappeared somewhere, probably to go flex his biceps in the mirror or use eye black to write "John 3:16" on his face.

I was suddenly seized with inspiration, and it was divine. My plan for revenge coalesced with my knowledge of the contents of Marcy's purse and the perfect window of opportunity.

"Give me your notepad!" I shrieked at Marcy.

She unzipped her stonewashed denim pocketbook and handed it to me. A bubblegum-colored pen was threaded through the spirals. I opened the notepad to a fresh page.

In big letters, I wrote, "IF YOU LIKE THIS CHURCH, YOU LIKE %$#%^^% *^&*(&^^* AND &^%^*%&*!"

(Except I used the real words.)

Marcy read it, shocked that I had written such a filthy and scathing accusation, and then started to laugh. I joined her, thrilled with my rebellion and creativity.

I tore off the paper. Crumbling it into a little ball, I tossed it into the plexiglass booth and sat back down with Marcy and Sissy.

Todd returned to the booth a few minutes later. He noticed the crumpled paper immediately. Marcy and I tried to play it cool as he read it. I was disappointed he didn't react visibly to the note's contents.

I was very interested in his thoughts since he did indeed like this church and therefore liked doing that thing to those things.

Todd walked out of the booth and over to us. My stomach felt like it dropped into my feet. I realized I was not as covert as I had assumed. Eyeing Marcy, he said, "Can I look in your purse?"

Marcy handed it to him wordlessly. It did not occur to any of us to say no.

He unzipped it and took out her notepad.

"Hmm. Same paper," he said.

He scribbled with her pen on a blank page, "and same pen."

We were silent.

"You kids are going to have to come with me."

Go with him? Where? Without calling our parents? What was going to happen to us? I knew I had done something wrong, but this wasn't right. We were trapped.

The shame, rage, and fear that had been building inside of me broke free. I had to get to Mama. I took off in a sprint, leaving Marcy and Sissy behind.

"Run, Heather!" one of them yelled.

Although terrified, I was exhilarated by their optimism. I ran as fast as I could, even though my shorts had ridden up my chubby legs and disappeared into my butt by the third stride.

In fact, I ran so fast that, under different circumstances, Todd might have given me a high five.

Since Todd was blocking the front exit, I detoured through the gym's side door. I wound my way through the educational building and ended up in the old chapel. I hit the bar on the double door at full speed, melting with relief when I found it unlocked.

Once outside, I ran around the back of the church and through our neighbor's back yard just in case Todd was waiting on me up front.

The things I had accused the church lovers of doing were only vigorous activities every married couple in the congregation already enjoyed (or endured) on a regular basis. More regular, in fact, if it was someone's birthday or the kids were away at camp.

I was still wrong to do it. I knew this, but I also knew every sad and bad feeling I experienced at church had threatened to erupt for years. And now, I had gotten myself in trouble without resolving a thing.

The last of my rebellious courage collapsed as I pounded up the flight of stairs outside our tiny house. By the time I opened the front door, I felt nothing but anguish.

Mom was washing dishes. "Mama! I did something bad," I cried.

"I wrote a dirty note, and Todd found it. He said he wanted all of us to go with him somewhere. I ran away, but he has Sissy and Marcy!"

"*Heather!*" she gasped. "What in the *world*, child?"

Even in her exasperation, Mama didn't sound any angrier

with me about this than she did any other time I'd been in trouble. A little of my anxiety abated. She dried her hands and shoved her feet into her sandals.

"Let's go," she said.

On the short walk over, I tried to explain what I did.

"I wrote it because they're a bunch of snobs! They don't even like us because we're poor!"

Mama did not speak. I feared she was starting to get wound up, like a tornado siren in an approaching storm. I tried a different tactic.

"Mama, I am so sorry. Please don't make me go talk to Todd."

"Heather, we have to go over there," she said, irritated. "They have your sister."

She opened the door to the Family Life Center. Todd was waiting for us. Thankfully, Marcy and Sissy were sitting in a booth.

"What's going on here?" demanded Mama.

"Your daughter wrote this note and dropped it where I could find it," said Todd, handing it to Mama.

She read it and gave me a Look.

"Heather," Mama said. It was an imperative.

"I'm sorry I wrote the note," I told him, not making eye contact. I made no attempt to explain my actions.

It's not like I could tell him the truth, that he was just a convenient target, a beefy congregational cog with a whistle around his neck, representing everything I didn't like about my religion.

Todd seemed satisfied. "I accept your apology," he said.

I exhaled, glad it was over and honestly, grateful for his forgiveness. I knew I had done a sinful thing. In my head, I promised God I wouldn't try to avenge our poverty again.

It wasn't Todd's fault we were poor.

It was his fault, though, that the only attention he'd ever given a group of needy kids was disciplinary.

I tried to shut down that little voice in my head. I knew that voice was a bad one. Maybe it was even the devil trying to tempt me into staying mad and writing notes to everyone in the church directory.

Mama gestured to Marcy and Sissy to gather their things.

Todd stopped them. "Before you got here," he said to Mama, "I took the girls to my office. I called Pastor Bryant and explained to him what happened. He wants to talk to all of you."

I was aghast. Now we were going to have to talk to the *preacher*? But I had already apologized!

"You took the kids to your office?" asked Mama. "Why? Heather's the one who wrote the note." Mom was not pleased.

"Well, I wasn't sure of that at first," he said lamely.

"Are you girls okay?" Mama asked Marcy and Sissy. They nodded.

"Do you want to go talk to the preacher?" Mama said, mostly to me.

Mama commandeered Todd's blustery authority with a single question by asking, not demanding. She had gifted me autonomy. I loved her for making me visible.

"I guess so."

All of us followed Todd to the pastor's study.

Pastor Bryant was sitting behind a big cherry desk. He was wearing a polo shirt and khakis, dressed more casually since it wasn't Sunday.

I thought he was nice. He would shake everybody's hand after service, not just the adults, and I liked him for that. If he knew my name, though, I was unaware of it.

He gestured for us to sit down. As we made ourselves comfortable, I noticed Sissy looking past him with interest. The set of the church's weekly TV show was visible. The background featured a gentle pastoral scene meant to soothe and uplift the viewer.

I was not uplifted. There were approximately 170,000 homes in the greater Knoxville area. I was here to apologize to the man who was broadcast into most of them.

My anxiety had returned, and my heart started to pound. I just wanted to get this over with. Pastor Bryant opened his mouth to speak.

I didn't hesitate. "I'm really sorry," I said quickly, not giving him a chance to start.

"Can you tell me what happened?" Pastor Bryant asked. He smiled reassuringly, the same way he did on TV.

This was my chance. Dare I lash out at him, tell him my deepest hurts, the ones inflicted by the people who called themselves Christians?

I focused my attention on the little embroidered logo on his shirt pocket so I wouldn't have to look him in the eye. Pastor Bryant's clothing was not ostentatious, but his casual outfit was still newer and more expensive than any of Daddy's work clothes.

My eyes shifted to Pastor Bryant's hands, folded paternally on the desk. His wedding ring was tasteful and elegant. I doubted he had ever had to pawn his wedding ring to pay bills like both Mama and Daddy had. Mama lost her engagement diamond that way.

My decision was instantaneous.

Pastor Bryant was a nice man, but he would not understand.

"The note was my idea," I said, "we were just goofing around and thought it was funny. I'm really sorry. I know it was a sin. We'll never do it again."

Marcy and Sissy mumbled in agreement, just to say something. They had both been dragged into this unfairly, especially

Sissy. She hadn't even seen the note. Even if she *had* seen it, she probably would have needed help sounding out the compound words. At school, her grade still wrote on large-lined manila paper.

And Marcy didn't really do anything, either. She had only acted as an office supply store.

"I'm happy to hear you say that," Pastor Bryant replied. "Everybody makes mistakes sometimes. God forgives you, and so do I."

I wondered if Todd had read the note to him or just summarized it. Thinking about Todd reading my emphatic opinion aloud to Pastor Bryant made me want to die from embarrassment.

Based on Pastor Bryant's response, I assumed Todd had skipped some details.

For instance, I was not asked why I harbored such animosity towards these good Southern Baptists.

Pastor Bryant stood up to shake our hands.

"I'm glad we had this talk. I'll look forward to seeing you all on Sunday."

I was relieved and disappointed at the same time. I wasn't going to have to explain my actions, but I wasn't going to get the chance to, either.

We exited the study, leaving Todd behind. He lingered, perhaps looking for praise for handling the situation. Hopefully, he wouldn't be congratulated on his ability to detain innocent children in the name of Jesus.

That was no way to be rewarded with a spot on the weekly TV program.

I trudged home behind Mama, Marcy, and Sissy. The weight of the day fell heavy as I walked. Once inside, Mama called Marcy's dad, telling him what happened and assuring him Marcy didn't do anything wrong.

After Marcy left, I went into the bedroom and shut the door. Depression crushed me. I knew there was one thing left to do, and it was going to be the hardest thing of all.

I was going to have to explain myself to Daddy.

Shame clawed at my heart. Daddy would know that I not only used bad words, but I used bad words as weapons aimed at people I was supposed to love.

Daddy did not use bad words. He thought they were coarse and unloving and did not honor the Lord. The thought of seeing disappointment on his face reduced me to tears again. I could not bear it.

The lesson was obvious. *A church can be full of jerks, and sometimes, you're the jerk.*

I cried for hours, grieving my actions but also grieving the treatment we had received. By the time the sun went down, my head hurt, and my voice was hoarse. I sat in the dark, brokenhearted.

I heard Daddy come home. There were murmurings from the living room. Mama was telling him what had happened. I was grateful I would not have to explain things from scratch.

Eventually, there was a knock on the door. Daddy came into the bedroom and sat on the bed beside me.

"Daddy, I'm so sorry."

"I know you are, Heather Pooh."

"Is God mad at me?" I asked, my voice cracking.

What I really meant was, *are you?*

Daddy was infinitely patient, loving, and gentle. He was the best and closest representation of God I had, far more real to me than any Bible story I had read. In fact, Daddy might as well have been God, as important as he was in my life.

If he was angry with me, I didn't think I could handle it.

He wrapped his long arm around me and held me close. Fresh tears fell from my eyes and wet the front of his shirt.

"God's not mad at you. He knows you're sorry. The Bible says He won't even remember what you did because you said you were sorry."

I nodded with my face pressed into his chest, transferring snot from my nose to my forehead. His answer matched what I had learned in Sunday School.

"Do you still love me, Daddy?"

Much like my theological question, I already knew the answer in my head but did not yet feel it in my heart.

"Of course, I still love you, Pooh Bear," he said cheerfully. "There is not a single thing that could ever happen that would make me stop loving you."

His deep radio voice reverberated in his chest, soothing me. My heart began to mend.

"Do you promise?" I asked, confident of the answer but wanting to hear it aloud just the same.

"I promise," said Daddy.

I still did not have the answers as to why there was so much Christian hypocrisy, and I was too exhausted to bring it up. But for now, I felt okay.

"Mama made some supper," he said. "Let's get us something to eat."

I followed him out of the bedroom and into the kitchen. My eyes squinted from the light in the rest of our home. I stumbled over to the roll of paper towels and tore off one to blow my nose.

Mama had cooked fried potatoes, pinto beans, and cornbread. She loaded up a plate and set it in front of me, kissing the side of my head noisily.

It was a good meal, eaten in fellowship, served without judgment.

This was a table where Jesus would sit and eat.

On the house.

Even though my plan for revenge backfired that day, I

vowed to remember how I felt. I had taken my best shot as a ten-year-old, but it wasn't enough. Maybe by the time I was an adult, I would know how to use more loving tactics to effect change in a lasting way.

I smothered my taters in ketchup, hopeful for the chance.

A church can be full of jerks, but one day, you will be a grown-up who can do something about it.

MANIFEST DESTINY

"Mom, can I stay home from school today?" I asked one morning.

Long before the concept of 'mental health days' entered the cultural zeitgeist, my mother was a champion of letting her kids stay home every once and awhile, away from the demands of the classroom. We called it "laying out" in our house.

"Why?"

"I just need a break," I said, giving my usual reason. Some days, the routine was too much. Schoolwork, recess, navigating the class bully, cafeteria corn dogs that were baked and not fried, homework.

Also, hating the feeling of getting up when it was still dark outside, never feeling rested and already being reliant on coffee in elementary school, having to do calisthenics in gym class while listening to a scratchy record calling me a Chicken

Fat, feeling anxious before timed math assessments, worrying about an audibly rumbly digestive system after lunch, being sad over not having money for the book fair, dreading being chosen classroom monitor when the teacher left the room, knowing the class butthead would test my boundaries.

Mama didn't have much of a childhood herself, having been born into a large family and forced into childrearing by default. Despite our lack of monetary resources, though, Mama tried to give us better than she had in every possible way.

"Okay, you can lay out, but we've got to go to Woodruff's to pay on the washer and dryer."

An incredible turn of events! A day off from school and a trip to downtown Knoxville, too? Downtown was one of my favorite places. I was giddy with excitement.

"Go ask Sissy if she wants to lay out, too," said Mom.

Sissy did indeed want to lay out. A brilliant child with a certain type of rude health, Sissy could have missed three days of school a week and still excelled.

This might have been because she was born at Knoxville's only teaching hospital. It was a place where everyone was treated regardless of ability to pay, but in exchange for cheap treatment, babies were less delivered than *caught*. As a newborn, Sissy was undoubtedly inspected quickly, like a factory package of chicken cutlets, and then sent to the nursery for a leisurely twelve hours of acclimation before discharge.

Being delivered there was barely a step above being birthed on the floor of the county health department, but it did endow Sissy with a haleness of which I was envious. I had been born at the Catholic hospital, surrounded by nurturing nuns, introduced to the world wearing a pink ruffled onesie and matching booties. Now I was paying for it with eczema and nervous fidgeting.

We quickly ate bowls of cereal, caught the bus, and headed downtown. The bus let us off on Gay Street, downtown's main hub. In the '80s, downtown Knoxville was very busy during the day, between the government businesses, department stores, and restaurants.

After 5 pm, it became a ghost town. The idea of missing the last bus home in the evening and being left alone in the empty city gave me nightmares. I was too old to hold onto Mom's hand, but I made sure to stay close to her as we made our way to Woodruff's.

We walked slowly down Gay Street, stopping to look in each storefront. My favorite was the Delta Air Lines office. They had a model plane in the front window, tilted as if in takeoff. I wondered what it would be like to sit in their modern, sophisticated office and plan a trip to a big city.

We also paused in front of Kimball's Jewelers, taking in their beautiful window display of watches and diamond earrings.

Mama sighed, no doubt thinking of her half-carat engagement ring, which had been lost to the pawnshop a few months before. Mama only owned a handful of jewelry as it was. Her engagement band had been thick and doubled as a wedding ring. Despite having pierced ears, she rarely wore earrings, or necklaces.

Her only concession to frilly femininity was inexpensive cocktail rings, and even those were often out of reach financially.

My maternal grandmother had been buried wearing Mama's favorite cocktail ring, a faux sapphire surrounded by enough cubic zirconia to repave the streets of Heaven.

The ring was a special token of love. Mama would not have surrendered her fancy jewelry to just any decedent. From a practical standpoint, it didn't make sense. What would a recently passed neighbor or coworker need her favorite bauble for? Showing it off to the Lord? There weren't any coronation balls up there.

My late grandmother, however, had spent part of her childhood in a tent city in Heber Springs, Arkansas. She was later committed to a state psychiatric hospital due to schizophrenia and spent her last years living in a nursing home, dying at the age of 57 from leukemia. She had grown up with even less than Mama. Mama loved her fiercely.

If anybody deserved to meet Jesus wearing Mama's best, it was my grandmother.

Eventually, we finished looking at jewelry and made our way into Woodruff's. Woodruff's was a Knoxville landmark, selling appliances and furniture downtown for over a century. It was full of lovely pieces but didn't feel inaccessible to the average shopper. Best of all, they had a payment plan that allowed families like ours to purchase items over time.

"Mom, can we ride the elevator?" I asked as soon as we walked into the store. I faked a little cough so the salespeople wouldn't think I was truant.

"After I make my payment," she replied.

My favorite part of visiting Woodruff's was taking the elevator and greeting the elevator operators. Watching them close the iron gate and push the buttons that took us to other floors was fascinating.

There was a barstool in the corner where the operators sometimes rested. I was always tempted to plop down on it for a front-row seat of the action. Observing the layers of concrete that separated the floors and watching them slide past me was better than a movie.

We walked past the furniture and into the back of the store, where the service desk and appliances were. My other favorite thing to do at Woodruff's was to open the new refrigerators and inhale the smell of the new plastic while Mama paid her bill. Mama didn't mind my long sniffs as long as I stayed close by. The employees, on the other hand, had different preferences.

That day, a beautiful set of china was on display next to the service desk, forty-five pieces in all. Pastel periwinkle, blush, and soft yellow flowers were printed on each item. The flowers were kissed by delicate pink butterflies and highlighted by backgrounds of cloud white. Mama and I stopped in our tracks, enchanted by its loveliness.

There were dinner plates, salad plates, elegant cups and saucers, a creamer pitcher, a container for sugar, a serving dish, and weird, shallow bowls that wouldn't hold even a fistful of Rice Krispies.

"Mom, what's that bowl thing?" I asked, pointing gingerly in its direction, and taking care not to touch it. Another one of her Woodruff's rules was to *look with your eyes, not with your hands.*

"That's called a soup plate," she said. "That's how fancy people eat their soup, out of a soup plate."

I nodded my understanding. If Kentucky Fried Chicken expected me to eat all their food with a spork, even if the spork tines punctured the roof of my mouth with every bite of mashed potatoes, I suppose fancy restaurants could serve steaming hot soup on plates. It made sense, I guess, even though it was rife with potential disaster. Gourmet dining was dangerous.

I read aloud the sign in front of the display.

"Enter to win this forty-five-piece fine china set. Drawing held at closing time."

"Well, I'm gonna enter that," said Mom. "I might just win us some fiiiiine chiiiiiina." Her voice drew out the vowels to be funny, to infuse the day with a little more excitement, but she did not smile as she said it.

I had been Mama's emotional weathervane since birth. This was not a job I had volunteered for, but there was no question I was an astute barometer. Mama often acted gregarious, even when depressed. She was long practiced in not getting her hopes up, seeing as how life started out tough and stayed that way.

I knew she was feeling weighed down by our poverty today. She wore her buoyancy like a raincoat, but it was less protective when confronted with tangible reminders of bounty like pretty china or diamond jewelry.

I tried to prop her up the only way I knew how. I hugged her affectionately.

"Go for it, Mama!"

She scribbled her info on an entry slip and folded the paper in half, then in half again. Maybe the paper's accordion texture would feel different than the other slips to the hand of the person who picked the winner. Maybe it would give her the edge.

That was Mama, perfectly distilled. She was different and wanted it to show.

She dropped her entry into the box and stepped over to the service desk to make a payment.

"Go find your sister," said Mom over her shoulder.

Sissy was long gone but assuredly close by. I walked to the front of the store, knowing where I would find her.

Sissy was quiet for a kid and liquidly skinny like a river otter. She would use her stealth to sneak into Woodruff's storefront windows and insert herself into the vignettes. She liked to pretend she lived in whatever scene was on display. She felt equally at home in a living room decorated with over-stuffed floral loveseats as she did a summer-themed outdoor barbeque grill set.

I peeked around the edge of the display and saw Sissy relaxing comfortably in a recliner. Across from her was a handsome wooden cabinet that featured a large color TV. The TV wasn't plugged in. A cardboard mockup of a football game was taped to the screen instead.

Sissy stared intently at the screen, concentrating as if the Tennessee Volunteers were third and goal on a real play.

If the bystanders on Gay Street happened to take notice of

Sissy, they wouldn't realize what they were witnessing. They would see an unsupervised kid, cute, sure – but also grubby.

She certainly wouldn't be sitting there because Woodruff's asked her to. After all, she was dressed in dirty jeans and a hand-me-down shirt that was too big for her, exposing one of her shoulders. A kid hired to advertise a business in a store-front window would at least be wearing sequins. Probably tap shoes and sprayed curls, too.

They didn't know her like I did. Sissy was a deep thinker, deliberate, and creative. Daddy called her his 'speckled egg,' proud of her individualistic nature. She had marched to her own beat right from the start.

This was in great contrast to me. I longed to be part of a group of like-minded people working in tandem. In fact, I longed to be part of a tribe so badly that I often conflated togetherness with happiness, even if I didn't like the people I found myself tethered to, especially if I was related to them.

Sissy did not sacrifice herself in the same way. Instead of exposing herself to the dysfunction of extended family each holiday, for example, she was allowed to spend that time with a friend. She wasn't afraid to be alone, either, if she did not feel valued.

She simply made herself scarce to anyone who didn't take the time to appreciate her rare speckles.

"Come on, Sissy. Mom's looking for us," I told her.

She rested in the recliner for a few more seconds. There was something about the way she sat that suggested ownership over the whole tableau. Sissy seemed to radiate determination. I felt absolutely sure that one day, she would own a recliner in every color if that's what she wanted.

Her confidence was contagious. She believed she could, and she made me believe it, too. Woodruff's could make a fortune off her if they had the vision to hire her to be their contemplative hype man.

Mama was still busy at the service desk, so Sissy and I took the stairs to the second floor. The second floor was open in the middle so that one could look down at the action below. We felt adequately close to Mama since we could easily spot her auburn head from where we stood.

The second floor was full of pretty lamps and tables. Imitating Sissy, I fiddled with the switch on an elegant mauve ginger jar lamp. I pretended the lamp belonged to me and that I was going to use it to read a sightseeing guide of New York City.

The warm light lit up my face, even on this sunny day.

I wanted very much to have furniture like this in my house when I grew up. Trouble was, my confidence in this outcome was much closer to Mama's expectations than Sissy's.

The familiar sensation of anxiety knotted my stomach and made my face hot. Most kids my age wanted Barbie Dream Houses or Nintendos as much as I wanted a new lamp. When I grew up, I knew I'd have a chance to get a job to earn enough money to buy one, *maybe*. Mama and Daddy were both smart, and Daddy worked his fingers to the bone, and we still had a house full of third-hand furniture. A job was no guarantee of success.

My brain routed my anxiety into another familiar sensation, hollow acceptance. Adulthood, successful or not, was a long way away.

I prayed to God, feeling guilty before I even started. There were kids all over the world who were starving; we didn't have it so bad. I was a rotten sinner for even asking, but I did anyway.

Dear Lord, it's just that we don't have any pretty things, so please let us have more money and let me grow up and be rich and let Sissy be rich so we can help Mama and Daddy and P.S., please help the starving children. In Jesus' name, I pray, amen.

I hoped God would understand. My certainty in His patience and generosity varied based on who was around to give me an answer.

Sissy called my name, alerting me that Mama had finished making her payment. We hurried downstairs to meet her.

"Are you ready to ride the elevator?" Mama asked.

The beautiful ginger jar lamp had taken some of the glow out of my day.

"That's okay. I don't want to right now." I didn't feel like smelling the spotless new fridges anymore, either.

"You girls want some lunch, then?"

"Can we afford to go to McDonald's?" I asked. Even deep in my mental malaise, I was excited at the prospect.

"Sure," Mama said flippantly. "Why not? We're rich!"

Mama said this often. It was obviously sarcastic, but it was rooted in charismatic Christian theology. That flock believed the signs and wonders performed by the apostles still happened today. Miracles were real, and God empowered believers to perform them, like healing the sick or parting the Tennessee River to escape the football traffic at Neyland Stadium.

I think Mama secretly believed she could speak money into existence, or at least hoped she could. Perhaps her belief was no more than a superstitious hedge bet to cover her bases in case God didn't deliver a miracle proactively enough to suit her.

Or maybe it was her own heartfelt plea to God, wrapped in a brash and bold personality that was, after all, gifted to her by God. Maybe He understood her lifelong anguish and didn't expect perfection from her when she approached Him in prayer.

Maybe He just knew what she meant.

Either way, I was in no position to judge, seeing as how materialistic my own prayers were. Mama had a funny way of getting things done. I didn't always understand her motives, but I couldn't argue with results. A Happy Meal in my hands was a miracle, provided I didn't think too hard about the details.

After lunch, we walked around Krutch Park and Market Square and made our way back to the bus stop. I was glad we were leaving town in plenty of time before business ceased for the day.

As soon as we started home, a foggy dread settled on me. It had been a pretty good day off, but not especially good enough to have missed school. My favorite lay-out days included souvenirs, like library books or cheap lip balm from the drug store. The only memento today was a feeling of powerlessness.

By the time I climbed the stairs to the entrance of our house, I was ready for a nap. I curled up in bed, snuggling the blanky I was much too old for. I loved the drowsy moments before I fell asleep, no matter how I was feeling. No worry, no longing, no disappointment. There was nothing in my mind except the weighted quiet of rest.

I was awakened by the sound of the telephone. At first, I tried not to focus on Mom's voice, hoping to fall back asleep.

"Are you serious?" I heard her say.

I opened my eyes. This sounded like interesting news.

"Well ... okay. I sure will. I'll be by to pick it up as soon as I can."

Pushing aside my leftover sleepiness, I walked into the living room and sat down on the couch next to Sissy, who was watching cartoons.

"What's going on?" I asked.

"Girls!" Mama said, "I won that china set from Woodruff's!"

I was amazed. Had God answered my prayer?

"You really won it, Mama?" I asked.

"I sure did. I've got to go pick it up. I'm gonna have to ask your Mammaw to give me a ride. I can't carry all that home on the bus." She giggled with joy.

"That's so awesome!" I gave her a happy hug. "Can we use the soup plates?"

"Why sure, hunnnnny!" Mama said, gesticulating dramatically the way wealthy characters did on TV. "We're gonna be the fanciest people in town."

She switched to a British accent, pretending to be a butler.

"And what would you like for dinner tonight, Madame?" she said to Sissy, who chuckled. Mama's British butler sounded as Ozarkian as Mama did.

My mind immediately tried to calculate any cause-and-effect between our entreaties that morning and the fact that Mama had won. Who had God listened to? Me, who formally prayed, or Mama, whose conversations with God were not only expectant but, frankly, pushy? Or was it the sum of both?

And Sissy had exhibited plenty of self-confidence over the recliner at Woodruff's earlier. Maybe her certainty had radiated out far enough to reach the china set, too.

These were the kind of unanswerable and circular questions that drove my Baptist Sunday School teachers to drink (but never dance).

Regardless of the supernatural means of transaction, I counted it as a win for all of us. A set of china was by far the biggest and best lay-out day souvenir to date. I couldn't wait to eat fish sticks or a peanut butter and jelly sandwich off those magnificent new plates.

A small flicker of hope re-ignited in my soul. Maybe the answer was that God had given Mama a special anointing for enter-to-win drawings. If so, we could be in for a windfall of Biblical proportions. If Mama won even a quarter of all the drawings in Knoxville, Sissy and I wouldn't have to wait until we were grown to try to make things better.

I closed my eyes and mentally traced a map of all the businesses in the downtown area. Surely one of them would eventually hold a drawing for a big diamond ring to replace the one Daddy slipped on Mama's finger all those years ago. Or a trip to see the Statue of Liberty. Or a *new car*.

And who was to say that if Woodruff's held another draw-ing, this time for a pair of exquisite lamps, Mama wouldn't win again?

I whispered, "Thank you, God, Jesus, and the Holy Ghost."

The flicker of hope grew from a nightlight to a torchiere.

Trying to cover all bases, I topped off my prayer with the same audacity Mama had shown earlier.

"We're rich. Amen."

I couldn't argue with results.

WE HAD THE ARTISTE

"Hey, Daddy, what are you doing?" I asked, peeking over Daddy's shoulder as he sat at our small kitchen table.

It was December 1989. Daddy got home at a decent hour during the winter since the station was on the air from sunup to sundown.

"Just drawing, Heather Pooh."

Daddy's drawings were special. He never drew idly. Each piece was given as a gift, their subjects varied and specific to the recipient.

He considered it a privilege and a pleasure to make these gifts, believing God guided him in the process so he could encourage and minister to the receiver.

Only one thing annoyed him, and that was when someone requested – nay, *demanded* - a drawing.

A breathtaking rendition of a cardinal, stunningly red and incredibly realistic, had been bestowed on Mama one year for their wedding anniversary. The piece of art was cherished and had been well-cared for a long time. Unfortunately, though Mama regularly insisted Daddy make her more drawings, she only had the one.

"I don't know why you won't draw me something else!" she often pestered.

"Because, my dear," he'd say, "you have the *artiste*."

I knew how she felt. It was hard not to feel jealous of those who had been given drawings. Everyone adored Daddy, and there was never enough of him to go around. He was perpetually at work, and when he wasn't at work, we were often at Mammaw's house, where a dozen people clamored for his attention. Both Mama and I felt neglected in our own ways.

Acquiring one of Daddy's drawings was the obvious solution. Since I had decided a piece of his artwork was an adequate substitute, I thought it only sensible that he give me one. I considered it efficient parenting.

He had recently finished a sketch entitled *The Celestial Organ*. The drawing was his interpretation of a supernatural musical instrument and featured towering pipage and an uninterrupted circular keyboard. The organ represented the unrevealed beauty of Heaven; in this case, a dazzling instrument used to present infinite praise to a loving Creator.

This piece was the most fascinating and beautiful one yet.

Daddy drew it with a coworker in mind, preparing to gift it to him the next time they worked together.

As soon as I saw it, I wanted it. There was something about the bright colors and the organ's gold details that captivated me. Poppy orange, sky blue, vibrant orchid, apple green. The hues of spring burst forth vividly on the page, as resounding as a triumphant chord booming from the organ's pipes. I could almost hear it.

Is this what Heaven is like? I thought. I was an advanced reader, but I found much of the Bible confusing and boring. Only Jesus' red words and the passages describing Heaven's fancy jeweled walls interested me, but Daddy knew his Bible well. If anyone could draw an accurate picture of the afterlife, it was him.

I didn't think Daddy's coworker would appreciate it nearly as much as I would. I wasted no time, asking Daddy right away if I could have the drawing.

As expected, he said no. "It's not for you, Heather Pooh," he explained patiently.

Through observation, I had learned that endlessly haranguing Daddy sometimes worked.

"But Daddy," I began, "You've never drawn anything for me, and it's *so beautiful.*"

He started to speak but then said nothing. I saw an opening.

"And Daddy, I feel like I never see you anymore. Can't I at least have this picture?"

He sighed. I had pulled out the big guns, the Daddy Daughter .38 Special, aimed straight at his heart.

"Let me think about it, Pooh Bear."

In my haste, I had forgotten to advocate for Mama's next drawing along with mine. Too late now, though. She'd have to be on her own for this one.

The following morning, I discovered the drawing lying on my and Sissy's dresser. He had inscribed it simply, "To Heather, From Dad."

Love for him washed over me, but I was not as happy as I thought I'd be. I suspected it was because, deep down, I felt I had forced his hand.

However, now that I had one picture, I did not desire or require another, unlike Mama. My drawing was an adequate substitute when Daddy wasn't around but insignificant when he was home.

Back in our kitchen, I watched Daddy sketch for a minute. He was beginning a new piece. I didn't think I'd mess anything up if I asked my favor.

"Daddy, can I pick in your hair?" A request as weird as me.

"Okay," he said.

Daddy's hair was long, thick, and silver. He didn't wash it often as he believed shampoo stripped away its natural oils.

That ensured his hair stayed shiny and frizz-free, but it also left dandruff.

I was a peculiar kid and an anxious one. For whatever reason, scratching flakes off Daddy's scalp was as calming to me as gentle summer rain or a silent retreat might be to others.

I got Daddy's pink plastic hairbrush, which had been purchased from the drugstore dollar bin, and began my exploration.

"Are you excited about Christmas, Daddy?"

Christmas was next week. Although we never had a lot of presents to open at home, Sissy and I usually scored a few good ones at Mammaw's house. Plus, Mammaw's celebration lasted two days, a party with punch and finger foods on Christmas Eve and a traditional turkey meal on Christmas Day.

During the festivities, Mammaw's house would be filled with dozens of relatives, and her dining room table would groan with food. Late on Christmas Eve, we would open presents, and the front room would be covered in a rainbow of ripped wrapping paper. Sometimes an aunt or uncle, forgetting to buy ahead but feeling generous, would press a folded bill into my hand, filling me with delight.

"Of course, I am," he said, trying to hold his head as steady as possible as he drew a curved line on the paper.

"Me, too," I added, excited about the food and gifts but also about showing off.

My first semester of middle school had been a remarkable one. Thanks to Ms. Prescott, who was gracious with her time and attention, I fell in love with science, ecology, and politics. There was so much to learn!

I had many newly educated opinions to share about the Hubble telescope, chlorofluorocarbons, and apartheid. I was ready to stake my claim as an enlightened adolescent. Pondering the topics I might discuss with my older cousins, I quit talking and concentrated on Daddy's scalp.

Daddy and I enjoyed our projects in silence. I parted Daddy's hair in a zigzag, not only to make him look like a punk rocker but also to check for hidden dandruff. Satisfied I had removed all the flakes, I brushed his hair and fixed it into a braid. It made him look like a little girl, and I snickered.

"You look pretty, Daddy."

"I'm sure I do," he said matter-of-factly.

"I sure do love you," I said, kissing his cheek. I smelled his scalp's oils and the remnants of tobacco. He only wore aftershave when he preached, which hadn't happened in years.

"I love you too, honey. Now, why don't you go watch TV with Sissy so I can work on this picture?"

I capitulated, retreating into the living room, but I left his braid intact.

The next day, Mom came down with the flu. She was miserable.

"Why in the hell did I have to get sick right before Christmas? I never get sick!" said Mama.

This was true. Mama rarely fell victim to congestion or a croupy chest, unlike me. She even managed to skate by allergy season, somehow dodging the effects of pollen while the rest of us were sneezy and red-eyed.

Since we were on holiday break, Sissy and I took care of Mama for several days. I was tall enough to safely carry a load of laundry from our downstairs garage, and I knew how to make Cream of Wheat and sandwiches, so I assumed the role of responsibility for the house until Daddy got home from work each evening. I relished the chance to prove my maturity.

By the time Christmas Eve rolled around, Mom was feeling somewhat better. She had been nagged into calling the doctor and getting a prescription for antibiotics, which seemed to be helping.

I decided to wear my black stirrup pants and denim jacket to Mammaw's get-together. The only Christmas-colored item I owned was a fashionable red purse an aunt had bought me for my birthday. I threw the purse over my shoulder and looked at myself in the mirror. I looked pretty cute.

As a final touch, I added my New Kids on the Block pin to the edge of the pleather strap and declared my outfit complete.

I met the rest of the family in the living room.

"I'm ready, Daddy."

He said, "Girls, what would you think about staying here instead of going to Mammaw's house? What if the four of us have our own celebration?"

Had he gone crazy?

We had always celebrated Christmas Eve with Mammaw. I thought of all we would be missing, starting with the food. One of my aunts' signature dishes was meatballs bathed in a sauce that had a perfect kick of sweetness. Plus, Mammaw always purchased a huge deli tray. I loved to create big sandwiches piled high with meats and fresh cheeses and then skewer them with fancy toothpicks for stability. Creamy fudge, crunchy nuts, jewel-like green sparkling punch, and more. My stomach growled thinking about it.

And what about all of us unwrapping gifts at the same time in the living room? Even if we stayed home tonight and only had to wait until tomorrow to open our presents from Mammaw, I would miss tonight's party atmosphere, and that's what I liked best.

Every member of our clever, extroverted family was their most attractive at Christmas. I was drawn to them like a moth to lit plastic reindeer. Conversations would overflow from each room of the house, and I would flit from group to group, sometimes to participate, sometimes to listen. Eventually, my uncles and cousins would set up amps and play old Ventures and Elvis tunes while the rest of us danced. Sometimes, Daddy could be coaxed to play the piano for a song or two.

Close to midnight, I would leave Mammaw's house worn out from all the activity but having only the warmest feelings toward my family. Even the family members normally teeming with dysfunction managed to behave themselves for two nights of the year.

I usually wanted Daddy all to myself, but I had no intention of staying in our quiet little home tonight. Absolutely *none*.

"Daddy, *no!*" I shouted and burst into tears. "I want to go to Mammaw's house!"

I wasn't trying to be rebellious; I was just taken aback by Daddy's change of plans.

Something broke inside me, and my sobs turned into wails. I wasn't entirely sure why. Some of it was the stress from the past week, with Mama getting sick and us having to take care of her. But it was Daddy's decision to break with tradition after so many years that was most shocking. Mammaw would be greatly upset if she missed seeing Daddy. Staying home must have been incredibly important if he was considering hurting his mother's feelings.

Oddly, I sobbed for another reason, too. It was not a fully formed thought, but it tickled the back of my mind like a feather.

Things were changing. I was closer than ever to being an adult, to leaving home, to getting married, to starting my own family. Traditions that were essential right now might not be in the future, and I couldn't prevent that.

I continued to cry louder and with such force that Daddy put his arms around me.

Mama said, "Honey, it's not that big of a deal. We'll go to Mammaw's!" She sounded alarmed.

Still, I sobbed. I felt ragged and bad. Just like with the drawing, I was too selfish to respect Daddy's wishes. Though my feelings were injurious to the most precious person in my life, I could not bear to stay in the peaceful silence of that tiny little house surrounded by reminders of poverty. Not on Christmas.

Daddy walked me over to the sofa. My tears had tapered off, but only because I was nearing exhaustion. I pressed my face against the arm of the couch and said nothing. Occasionally, my chest would hitch, and I would bark out another sob. I did not understand why I could not be consoled.

After almost an hour of tears, Daddy bent down in front of the couch and took my hands in his. His gentle brown eyes were sad and resigned. He looked as though he understood he would experience many, many more adolescent outbursts in the years to come and that each one would try his patience.

"Okay, Heather Pooh," he said gently. "We'll go to Mammaw's house."

Again, I had gotten my way. Why didn't I feel better?

As soon as we pulled into Mammaw's driveway, which was overflowing with cars, I put the crying jag behind me. I really wanted to have a good time. Our family seemed brighter and more boisterous than usual. A new decade was around the corner, my uncles talked about playing more gigs in the new year, and an aunt proudly discussed her small payroll business. We all wondered if my cousin would propose to the girlfriend he had brought to the party. She had been to several gatherings already.

Once I had filled up on meatballs and butted into every conversation in the house, I made my way back to Daddy. He was talking music with his brothers and eating a sandwich made with pumpernickel bread. He was the only one of us who liked it.

"Shoo, Daddy," I interrupted him. "That bread smells like dirty armpits."

As always, he was a paragon of patience.

"Well, more for me," he said, taking another bite.

Sharing everything with children who viewed anything he possessed as their birthright must have been tiresome. At least he had pumpernickel bread all to himself.

Later, we opened our presents. Mammaw had gotten me a delicate wooden jewelry box and my aunt a necklace to go inside. Grown-up gifts for a woman-to-be.

I sat on the couch next to Mom, who had been fortifying herself with coffee the whole night. She looked tired. I was fatigued myself.

"Are we ready to go home?" I asked.

"Just about. Your Daddy's still talking to Mammaw. Did you have fun?"

I had eaten my weight in fudge and gotten some great presents. With all the people there, it felt like I had been to a dozen exciting parties, not just one. The opportunity never arose for me to analyze and debate global topics with my family, but that was okay. Everyone was just too happy to argue.

"Yeah. It's been a great Christmas."

On the evening of December 29, I was still revising my list of New Year's resolutions. Even a trip to the video store, which was a favorite, didn't hold my interest long. My list was top priority. I was eleven now and finally old enough for the same kind of formalized self-improvement I saw in every "women's interest" magazine.

Going on a diet was a must as I now wore a bigger size than Mama, which embarrassed me. I also recommitted myself to absolute scholarship at school, with the hope I might win a Governor's Award for my academic achievement. I liked the way I looked when I wore lip gloss and blush. Should I vow to wake up earlier to put on makeup?

Studying my Bible, practicing my clarinet more, not fighting with Sissy. There were many more resolutions to ponder, but I had time. The new year was still two days away. I fell asleep with my thoughts still swirling.

Sometime in the night, Mama shook me awake.

"Heather, I need you to wake up, baby." I was still processing her voice when she turned on my bedside lamp. I winced in pain from the light.

"Listen to me. I need you to call 911. Daddy's not breathing."

A bright blob of horror drenched me. I was instantly awake.

"What? He's not breathing?" I repeated, hoping I had misheard her.

"Can you do that for me?" Mama asked. She did not affirm my question, but her next words left no doubt.

"I have to give him CPR," she said and rushed back into their bedroom.

Preternaturally calm, I picked up the phone beside my bed. The phone happened to be close. Earlier, I had stretched its long cord from the living room to my bedroom to call Marcy. This bit of convenience did nothing to help mitigate the nightmare.

I did what Mama asked.

"911, what is your emergency?"

My heart started racing as soon as I heard the operator's voice. I took a deep breath and began to speak. Somehow, my voice did not tremble.

"We need help, please. An ambulance. My daddy is not breathing."

"What's your name?" the operator said sharply.

I told her. "Can you please send an ambulance? Our address is -"

She cut me off. Incredibly, she said, "Is your mother there?"

My heart slammed into the wall of my chest, pumping faster and faster. Did this awful woman think I was making a prank phone call?

Feeling a hundred emotions but unable to put voice to any of them, I thought of Daddy and squeaked out an answer.

"Yes, I'll go get her. But please send an ambulance."

As I dropped the receiver on the bed, I heard the operator inhale in realization. No prank caller would go get their mother. *I told you, stupid*, I thought to myself.

Our bedrooms were only steps apart.

Mama was bent over Daddy, who was sprawled across their mattress at a 45-degree angle.

"Mom, she needs to talk to you!" I said frantically.

"Oh, my God!" said Mama, sliding off the bed and running past me.

I forced myself to look at Daddy. He was wearing his

t-shirt and a pair of boxer shorts. I had never seen Daddy in his underwear. He was tremendously modest. I wished I hadn't seen him now.

"Daddy?" I said, shaking him. He did not respond. His eyes were open and unblinking, staring at the ceiling.

Feelings of terror and dread shot off in my brain like fireworks, the ones so close by you only hear the deafening boom long after the sparkle has gone.

It took every bit of my bravery to lean over the bed. I rested my head on Daddy's chest and listened to his heart.

Lub-dub, lub.......dub. Lubdublubdublub....dub.

Freshly terrified, I sprinted back into our bedroom to get Mama.

She was screaming at the operator. "Goddamn you! We need an ambulance!"

"Mama! Daddy's heart sounds funny!" I yelled in the background, wanting the operator to hear me.

"I'm giving the phone back to my daughter now. She has my permission," she said, handing it over.

"Hello?"

"What is your address?" the operator said, nonplussed.

I hated her.

Our address rolled off my tongue quickly. She repeated it back to me and told me the ambulance was on its way.

I hung up. Sissy was awake and had watched the interaction

between us and the operator without comment.

"Let's go, Sissy. We've got to go flag down the ambulance."

We didn't bother with shoes or coats, although Sissy wrapped herself in her blanky. I opened the door and beheld the cold December darkness. We carefully walked down the stairs and onto the driveway. The jagged concrete hurt my feet, but my only concern was the ambulance.

I grabbed Sissy's small shoulders and started praying, my fear temporarily shocked into retreat by the biting winter air.

"Dear God, please save Daddy. Please help him. Let him be okay. We love him so much, and we ask that you please help Daddy in Jesus' name, amen."

We said nothing after that. Time seemed both elastic and inexorable while we waited. There was only one thing that mattered, and yet, nothing mattered at all.

I shivered, and my bladder tingled with heaviness. Surely, this night couldn't be real. Only the pinnacle of irrationality would make sense at a time like this. I thought about wetting myself to warm up my feet. I eventually rejected the notion, trying to hang on to some dignity, wrapping myself in the need for it like the coat I wish I had.

After an unknown time, the ambulance arrived, pulling into our driveway without its lights or sirens on. I was bewildered and angry. My daddy's life hung in the balance. Was this not an emergency to them?

Two paramedics quickly got out of the ambulance and opened the back to retrieve the stretcher.

"Where are we going?" one of them asked.

I pointed upstairs. "There," I said.

His path to the staircase brought him close to me. As he picked up the back end of the stretcher, I grabbed the sleeve of his black nylon jacket.

"Please save my daddy," I said, tears clogging my throat for the first time since Mama had woken me up.

He looked at me mildly and said nothing. He and the other paramedic climbed the stairs and disappeared into our house.

Sissy and I waited a few more minutes outside on purpose. I had seen enough medical shows on TV to know they might be using paddles to shock Daddy's chest. I could not bear to watch his body arch and retract from the zaps of electricity. Our house was tiny, and there was nowhere to hide from what was happening.

Mama had no choice but to bear witness.

I tried to time our re-entry for when I thought the most brutal interventions would be over. Finally, I took Sissy's hand, and we walked upstairs. My body and brain felt numb as I pushed the door the rest of the way open. It had been left ajar by the paramedics.

Mama was sitting on our old green couch, silent. My eyes searched hers.

I knew instantaneously. The last time her thoughts affected me that quickly was when the umbilical cord was still attached.

The surrealness of the moment hit me squarely. Oddly, I felt nothing. It was as if someone had hit me in the chest with a baseball, but I was covered in pounds of padding.

I heard myself say, "He isn't ... is he?"

Mama nodded.

Although I outweighed her, I jumped onto Mama's lap, pressing myself against her like I did as a baby. The motion made the couch rock back and touch the wall. I held onto her tightly. I made the sound of sobbing, but it felt more like screaming.

The insulated padded feeling remained. There was no catharsis in my crying. I felt removed from my emotions the same way an actress might during a rehearsal coffee break.

Mom held me for a minute while she gathered Sissy to her.

"Girls, he was just too far gone," she said.

Daddy was too far gone. Too far. Now gone. The words danced in my head, a poem of insanity. My face crumpled again.

"What are they going to do with him?" I asked.

"They will take him to Berry's," she said. Berry's was a nearby funeral home, the one down the street from the cemetery where my paternal grandfather was buried.

"I asked the paramedics to fix your daddy so you can say goodbye to him while he's still... warm."

Mama paused before saying the last word. It was a deranged way to offer comfort, but what good were words right now? We had just endured a bomb blast. Mentally, we were standing in a smoking hole, ears ringing.

"Should I go in there now?" I needed her, or anyone, to tell me what to do. A grown-up telling a kid what to do was right and normal. Surely, a bit of order would help.

"Go on. I have to call your Mammaw and tell her," she said. How was Mama going to deliver that news? Fresh hysteria grabbed at me, but the insulation of shock once again kept the shrieking at bay.

I walked into Mama and Daddy's bedroom. Daddy was positioned on his side of the bed. His eyes had been closed, and his hands were folded over his stomach.

Someone had covered his lower half with the orange-and-white crocheted blanket Mama once won at a raffle. The colors were very cheerful. I wondered what we would do with the blanket after all this. If we kept it, could I ever touch it again?

Daddy looked peaceful and in order. I watched him for a minute. Nothing changed. Stillness and silence surrounded us. To my surprise, it was not burdensome. I was reminded of my visits to Daddy's radio station over the years. I felt like I was standing in one of the soundproof booths with the door shut, only able to hear my breathing.

"Oh, Daddy," I whispered.

The quiet embraced me, a caring companion.

My body, infused with an intuitive wisdom all its own, allowed the first trickles of grief to surface. Some of the insulated feeling slid off me as the hot flush of tears filled my eyes.

Lying in this bed, but gone from this world, was my greatest protector and encourager. The one who understood me the best and helped me understand things the best was now forever silent.

There would be no more appearances at school events or special candy treats from the corner convenience store. He would never again play a piano chord or draw with his colored pencils. He would never again be the last one to come to bed, and I would never again feel quite as safe falling asleep.

He would never know me as a grown woman, and he would never kiss my cheek on graduation day, at my wedding reception, or on a Thursday ever again.

I kissed him as I had a million times before.

"Thank you for being a good Daddy," I told him.

"I love you," I said, tears bathing my face as I turned to leave. It was the last time we were alone together, ever again.

The smithereens of my life lay beyond the door. I already knew the weight of the coming days would press on me hard, but I could not change it. I left the bedroom and crossed the threshold into the next act.

Mama was standing in the kitchen with the paramedics.

They were asking questions and writing down information. I sat at the table.

"Ma'am, can you tell me your husband's full name?"

She answered him slowly. She sounded dazed, like she had suffered a head injury.

"And what was his birthdate?" he asked, pen poised above his notebook.

Mama didn't say anything.

"Ma'am? His birthdate?"

All at once, she sunk to the floor in a faint while both paramedics grabbed her arms to cushion the fall. They maneuvered her into a chair. One of them attended to her while the other filled a glass with tap water.

She came to quickly. "Are you alright, ma'am?" he asked, and she nodded.

"We have just a few more questions, and then we'll get your husband's body to Berry's," he said gently. "Is your family close by?"

"My mother-in-law is on her way."

"Okay, that's good. Can you tell me your husband's birthdate?"

Mama was once again silent.

I was a heartbroken, grief-stricken middle-school kid in great need of solace. My wounds were raw and deep, the pain just beginning to emerge.

Yet, I was the only one there to help. My new role was apparent.

Maybe Mama could limp a little further if she leaned against me.

"September 4, 1941," I said, and my voice was clear and strong. "He was forty-eight."

The paramedics seemed relieved to move forward.

"Do you have his driver's license?" one asked, and I retrieved it from Daddy's wallet, which Mama had already gathered and placed on the kitchen table. Now, it was her wallet.

The paramedic with the notebook copied some info from Daddy's license, and I answered a few more questions. By then, the sun had begun to rise. On a normal day, Daddy would have already been on his way to work.

"Oh, God," said Mama, "I have to call the Nortons and tell them about your daddy."

Perry and Mary Norton owned the radio station where Daddy worked. They had known Daddy for years, professed to be devout Baptists, and professed to love Daddy deeply.

Perhaps they did, but Mama and I eyed their Christian love with suspicion. Daddy worked overtime every week, but his check was still small enough that Sissy and I qualified for free lunch at school. The Nortons also did not offer health insurance or paid time off. They were only truly generous with compliments and promises of promotion that never panned out.

Daddy had always been able to overlook his bosses' shortcomings, but Mama never could. She couldn't pay the utility bill with a check drawn from the bank of the Nortons' adulation.

I watched Mama walk back into my and Sissy's bedroom, where the phone was still on the floor. With her back to me, she picked up the phone, wedged the receiver between her ear and her shoulder, and dialed the Nortons' number.

One of them answered the phone.

"Tommy won't be in to work today," Mama said.

Whoever was on the other end asked why.

"He's dead," she said and hung up the phone.

She provided no further explanation. I knew exactly what she was thinking. They helped put Daddy into an early grave. I felt the same way.

Blankly, Mama said, "Mary started screaming when she heard the news."

I felt small and sinful but darkly satisfied that Mama had lobbed a grenade. I hoped they were also grieving from deep inside a smoldering crater.

The phone started ringing, but Mama ignored it. "I'll call them later," she said, and we waited for the rest of the family to arrive.

~

OUR FAMILY HURRIEDLY SCHEDULED the Receiving of Friends for New Year's Day and the burial for the day after, hoping to use the holiday advantage so more people could attend without missing work. The timing was terrible. Not only did it mean that we would all start the new decade in mourning, but also that Daddy would be laid to rest on January 2, Mama and Daddy's wedding anniversary.

For Mama, the whole burial process was one deep hurt after another. We couldn't afford to pay for Daddy's funeral outright, so Mama had to sign a contract to pay it off in installments. A few of our family members gave cash to help lower the balance, but one of those who donated tried to take over the arrangements. Mom put her foot down, explaining there was no need to bury Daddy in a coffin that cost as much as a Cadillac.

"I wish they would've spent that much money on him while he was still alive," she complained. "He could have used some new shoes for work. Lord, that man had so much pride."

That was true, but my only desire was for everyone to come together and stop squabbling. My family was great at disguising grief as anger. If they wanted Daddy to have an expensive casket, and Mama's buy-in shut everybody up for a while, so be it. Still, I was glad to see a little of Mama's spark return. She wasn't truly alive without a dragon to slay.

In the end, Daddy's body was displayed in a simple, inexpensive wooden casket. Several of us tucked notes or trinkets into it.

Before the service, I considered putting the drawing he gifted me into the casket. To do so would sting, no doubt, but wouldn't it be a just punishment? Daddy didn't want to give it to me in the first place. I had only wanted it as a substitution for him, but it turned out to be the final substitution.

Never sure about God's intentions, I thought it possible that He was teaching me a lesson. Daddy thought God had wanted him to draw *The Celestial Organ* for a friend. He disobeyed God and gave it to me instead. Now Daddy was in Heaven, and I was left with someone else's drawing. Maybe it was up to me to redeem the whole situation and repent by burying the thing permanently.

This type of supernatural conundrum was exactly the kind of thing I used to ask Daddy about, but now he was out of this world forever. I wondered what he was doing in eternity. Maybe he was playing a real celestial organ or breaking odor-free pumpernickel bread with Jesus. Surely it didn't smell like armpits in Heaven.

The decision was mine and mine alone. I was going to have to come to terms with my choices now Daddy was gone. It wasn't as easy as just finding a new spiritual advisor. I had already experienced eleven years of well-meaning but overwhelmingly single-minded church folk. They rarely had answers for my complicated musings. Daddy had been a needle in a haystack.

My mind whispered something. I wasn't sure if it was the Holy Spirit or my subconscious.

Maybe Daddy didn't know, but you did.

I remembered my inexplicable meltdown on Christmas Eve and Mama's unusual illness.

Had we known? Had we somehow known he was going to die?

Maybe the drawing was always for you, but God protected Daddy from knowing why.

I let the possibility stretch its legs in my brain, in my heart.

Pondering did nothing but create more questions, but it kept the drawing out of Daddy's casket.

The Receiving of Friends went on for hours, with almost 400 people stopping by to pay their respects.

I ultimately decided to add a hair clip I made Daddy to the casket. I had glued wooden letters from the five-and-dime store onto a barrette post for his last Father's Day gift. I told him I had made it for him in case he wanted to pull his long hair back out of his eyes, but mainly I made it because I loved crafts.

My gift was supposed to read, "#1 DAD," but there wasn't enough room for the entire phrase. Instead, it said, "1 DAD," which I guess was close enough. One dad was all I needed.

My contribution was special, but not so special I'd miss it if it were in the ground, like the drawing.

The clock read 8 pm. The drawing room was hot and stuffy from the number of mourners. For the first time that evening, no one was standing directly in front of Daddy's display. It was a good time to tuck my barrette into the casket.

I slid the barrette into the side of the coffin, close to Daddy's thigh, not wanting to touch him. I scrutinized the rest of his body and froze in disbelief when I got to his face.

One of Daddy's eyes had popped open.

Not all the way, but far enough to see more than a sliver of white sclera.

I was aghast. Disgusted. Horrified. Thankfully, Mom was close by.

"Mama!" I stage-whispered, gesturing frantically for her to join me.

I pulled her close and aligned her arms with mine. Together, we provided cover for Daddy's head.

"Daddy's eye is open," I muttered so as not to cause a scene. "It must be the heat in here."

Already laid low by grief and fatigue, I was torn between laughing and crying. Being the one who discovered the embalmer's sloppy job was a new kind of trauma and one I hadn't accounted for. I looked at Mom for guidance.

Her weariness and pain were visible. She met my gaze,

and I watched her decide between madness and mental management.

"Well, Tommy always said he'd try to come back if he could," she declared perkily.

We said nothing for a moment, then burst out laughing. The last few days had been an absurdity, a monstrosity, a nonsensical plot twist of the worst kind.

But the hardest part would soon be over unless Daddy's coffin shot out of the hearse tomorrow and fell on top of a puppy as a special anniversary tribute.

A choice had been made, at least for tonight. The next day, we would have to choose again. Then the next, and the next, and the next, until our anguish hopefully softened enough to mold into memory.

We couldn't change what had happened, but it was up to us to move forward. There was no going back.

We used to have the *artiste*, and now we had his sketch pad.

STRIKING OIL

For better or worse, one of Mama's first decisions after Daddy died was to pack up and go live somewhere else. Although she was intent on letting Sissy and I finish the school year where we had started, she was ready to move on from our tiny house, the last place we had lived as a family of four.

I had mixed feelings. I was loathe to leave my middle school as I had finally found a teacher who truly mentored me, along with a group of geeky friends who were passionate about conservation and scholarship. On the other hand, our home and neighborhood would forever be associated with loss. No matter how many times we rearranged the furniture or avoided riding past where Daddy used to work, South Knoxville was sullied by his death.

There was another reason to consider moving. We were no longer the same as before he died. Now we were traumatized and in deep mourning, and so were our relatives. Moving meant a fresh start, a chance to leave behind some of the grief and the emotional baggage that came with it.

There were events and parties and sleepovers and dinners going on all around us where people were having good times, not sitting in darkened living rooms staring at TV, trying to keep their minds off a loved one's passing. Our family's sorrow was radioactive and so psychically strong it was sticky.

We were rebuilding from scratch. The opportunity to reinvent ourselves was there if we got far enough away from the fallout of lamentation.

At first, Mama wanted to leave Tennessee altogether and move back to Arkansas, where she grew up. Most of her large family still lived there, and they welcomed the idea.

My protest was immediate.

"Mom," I said passionately, "there is no way I'm going to leave all of Daddy's family to go live in the buttcrack of America."

Two of my favorite aunts, Mama's sisters, did live there, but most of what I had experienced about the state overshadowed the good.

The only place that made me feel poorer than Tennessee was Arkansas. The highway from Little Rock to Pine Bluff, where a lot of our family lived, was lined with rickety houses and ugly farmland. A ramshackle house with a leaky roof and copperheads as neighbors wouldn't be a step up, even if it turned out to be the nicest shack in town. If rich people lived in Pine Bluff, I'd never met them.

There were also likely fewer educational opportunities there. I had recently returned from a trip to Middle Tennessee State University, where Ms. Prescott's father was president. As a special treat for my school's scholar bowl team, we had stayed overnight in the beautiful presidential home and toured the campus.

Our dinner conversation had been as genteel as the rosette pats of butter that were served with the bread. It didn't matter that my ability to smear cold butter was too challenging for my dexterity, resulting in a shredded roll, or that the fanciest thing I had packed was a Bart Simpson t-shirt. This was the kind of life I aspired to.

"Do they even know how to read in Arkansas?" I asked sassily.

"You better watch that smart mouth," said Mama. "You know your Aunt Lola is an English teacher."

Lucky for me, Mom dropped the idea of moving out of state and started looking in other parts of Knoxville.

Remarkably, the only reason we could move in the first place was that the federal government had come to our rescue.

Since Sissy and I were minors, and since Daddy wouldn't be using his social security benefits now, the feds awarded us stipends to be distributed monthly until we turned 18.

Between the survivors' benefits and Mama's job, we ended up with almost $600 more a month than Daddy had earned working overtime each week. This was an astonishing amount of money, literal pennies from Heaven. Not for the first time, I promised myself I'd register as a Democrat when I was old enough to vote.

Our family owed the Roosevelts a lot.

"If we're going to move, I need to find a new job," Mama told us. "I can't drive all over creation just to work in the floral department."

Mom had worked part-time at our nearby grocery store for a couple of years to help supplement Daddy's income. A few of Mama's friends babysat us during that time since we were too young to stay by ourselves.

"Are you thinking about teaching again?" I asked, already knowing the answer but trying to be polite. Before her job at the grocery store, she had tried substitute teaching at my cousins' high school.

Unfortunately, education had changed a lot in the years since she earned her degree. The students were ruder and more disrespectful than she remembered.

"Hell, no!" she answered. "I can't handle them kids no more."

I was relieved for the Knox County school system but also for myself. I didn't want to share her in that way. I was already missing one parent.

"Well, who would stay with us if you were at work?"

"Do you think you and Sissy are ready to stay by yourselves?" Mama asked.

I was happily surprised by her question. I was pleased she would trust us enough to be alone without burning down the house or opening the door to a stranger who might kidnap us or sell us encyclopedias.

"Am I old enough?" I asked, just to be sure. My confidence was never more lacking than when I thought of trying something new.

"You're almost twelve. I was changing your Uncle Jed's diapers and cooking dinner at your age," she said, giving me yet another reason to steer clear of Arkansas.

"Okay," I replied. Things were settled. All at once, I seemed to be knocking on the door to adulthood. It was the start of my reinvention.

"You'll be fine," said Mom. "Just don't drink any wine coolers or let Sissy ride her bicycle inside the house."

These were the lowest of bars to clear, but for some reason, Mama's standards did not inspire confidence.

We began our search for a new home in earnest. The survivors' benefits had changed our lives. For the first time in her life, Mama considered purchasing instead of renting, in theory, at least. We had no savings for a down payment on a house, but Mom was anxious to move, so she began to explore other options.

She toyed with the idea of buying a mobile home after visiting her niece's place across town. Mobile homes, or trailers, as they were also known, used a different type of financing than a regular house. Trailers didn't require big down payments, which was a plus, but their monthly payments were considered downright usurious to anyone who understood the basics of compound interest. And unlike houses, trailers didn't generally appreciate in value. They just slowly decayed in place or got lifted into another county by a tornado, whichever came first.

Also, most trailer park lots were rented; they weren't available for purchase. So, even if someone managed to pay the home off, they would still have to pay a fee for the privilege of parking it on a brown patch of grass every month, without cease, until they went to that great trailer park in the sky.

The whole manufactured house business was a mix of the worst features of both owning and renting property, and yet the people at the top were making money hand over fist.

Notably, Mama majored in early childhood education, not economics.

She was blown away by my cousin Amy's tidy blue double-wide. From the outside, it looked like a real house, complete with landscaping and country white shutters.

"You girls need to see this place!" Mama said breathlessly after her visit. "It's got two bathrooms and a washer/ dryer hookup and new carpet. And the trailer park has a big pond and a fountain at the entrance!"

I had to admit, that didn't sound like any trailer or trailer park I'd seen. Most local trailer parks were decrepit and filled with long rectangular dwellings that looked like shipping containers. The trailers were usually old and rusty and surrounded by dirty buckets and greasy transmission parts.

Most residents looked as broken down as the cars up on blocks. A trailer park was usually a place to escape from, not to, a place where the police might begin their investigation if they were searching for a serial arsonist who eschewed trousers or a drug aficionado who also loved *Hee Haw*.

Amy was the most cosmopolitan of the family, though, so if she chose to live in a trailer park, it must be a nice one.

"I haven't told you the best part," Mama continued. "All the streets are named after the TV show *Dallas*. And their clubhouse is a replica of Southfork!"

Now I was definitely interested. I loved watching *Dallas* with Mammaw at her house on Friday nights. Every season, the sequins and the shoulder pads at the Oil Baron's Ball got shinier and bigger, and there were always fights during the wedding receptions where someone would get punched and end up in the Southfork pool.

"Where does Amy live?" I asked, hoping it wouldn't have anything to do with J.R., the character I loved to hate.

"Miss Ellie Drive!" said Mama excitedly. Miss Ellie was J.R.'s saint-like mother, the moral compass who held the Ewing family and the Southfork ranch together. I was happy for Amy.

Somehow, the fact that the streets were named after fictional rich people elevated it in my eyes. A trailer park that was billionaire-adjacent seemed almost as ritzy as the ranch itself, especially compared with the tiny house we had lived in with Daddy.

"When can we go see?" Mama's exuberance was hard to ignore.

Soon, we were in the car on our way to Amy's. Clayton Homes, a giant in the mobile home business and a Knoxville mainstay, had named the trailer park with an obvious nod to the show. A tasteful forest green sign marked the entrance.

"Southfork - A Mobile Home Community" was carved into the wood.

We made the turn into the park, and my jaw dropped. The road bisected two large ponds, one ringed with a walking trail, the other full of ducks swimming around a fountain that shot twenty feet in the air.

To my left, I saw a gazebo and a tennis court. A tennis court?!? Only rich people played tennis! For the first time in my life, I imagined myself playing, although in a skirt much longer than anything I'd ever seen Chris Evert wear, to flatter my thighs.

The most incredible sight was the clubhouse. It *was* a replica of the Southfork Ranch. It had two stories, white siding, black shutters, and columns in the front.

"Holy crap!" I yelled in excitement, momentarily forgetting my aspirational elite, educated status.

Mama stopped the car in front of the clubhouse. She looked at me, pausing dramatically.

"You know what else they have?" she asked.

"What?"

"A *pool*," Mama said, and Sissy and I whooped happily.

"They really have a pool?" I screeched, and Mom drove into the clubhouse parking lot, so we could see. We tumbled out of the car and walked past the manicured island where a bank of neat, identical post boxes sat next to a soda machine.

The fence to the pool was locked, but Sissy and I pressed our faces between the black iron slats. The pool was surrounded by matching beach loungers. Numerical mosaic tiles marked off the depths and added more decoration. The water was a clear, shimmering turquoise.

My aquatic experience had been limited to dips in a couple

of large community pools and East Tennessee's cloudy lakes. I couldn't swim, but I could float, which seemed like all the training I needed to lounge in this oasis.

Now, I understood the difference between a trailer park and a mobile home community.

"Mom, can we live here?" I asked, still looking at the water.

"I'm working on it, Heather Pooh."

Heather Pooh. That was what Daddy had called me the most. I had managed a whole hour without thinking of him.

The sadness crashed back into me like a foamy wave made by a cocky teenage boy cannonballing into the pool. Grief had been there the whole time, waiting to drench me.

I tried to imagine living in this rich person's trailer park until my melancholy mood receded. Moving sounded better with every passing minute. I began to dread returning to our tiny house, resigned to the fact that the stifling sadness knew its way around there much better. It never hesitated to make itself at home.

Surely, God wouldn't tease us with this possibility and then not deliver. Surely, He would give us the chance to rebuild better since He had demolished our old safe places.

"Did I tell you Amy put her baby grand piano in the front window?" said Mama. "It looks just beautiful."

"I want to go see!" I begged, and we drove to Amy's for the tour.

⌒

I RETURNED FROM MARCY'S house one afternoon after a sleepover and found Mom on her tippy toes, peering into the kitchen cabinets above the sink.

"Hey, Mom, what are you doing?"

She turned to face me. She was elated.

"I'm looking to see what we need to pack. I picked out a trailer today!"

"At Southfork?"

"Yes!" she said, and I squealed with joy.

"What does it look like?" I wanted to know.

"Well, it's a singlewide…not as fancy as Amy's, but you and Sissy each get your own room, and the two of you get a bathroom."

I was speechless. "I get my own *room*?!?"

Sissy hovered around Mom, ready to speak her piece.

"Yes, but Sissy came with me today, and she got to pick hers out first. She got the one with the bay window."

I didn't mind. Sissy had already endured years of my over-sized hand-me-downs and forced makeovers where I covered her face in toothpaste to 'open her pores.' I was happy she was getting an upgrade.

"That's okay. I get my own room!" I yelled, then danced around the house. I flapped my arms in a joyful rendition of the Funky Chicken. Soon, Mama and Sissy danced with me.

"What street is our trailer on?" I was hoping she'd say Suellen or Pam, who were my favorite characters on the show.

"Southfork Drive," said Mama, doing the Twist.

"Oh," I said, a tad disappointed.

On the other hand, I considered, "At least it's not J.R. Drive."

J.R. was the type who'd tear down an orphanage if it were sitting atop an oil well. I was glad the post office would not associate us with a man like that.

"I guess I'd better start packing, too," I said, kicking like a Rockette all the way into the bedroom. I wished we didn't have to take anything and could just leave our worn-out things behind. The trailer was going to be the nicest place we'd ever lived. God had not let us down.

A new beginning was upon us, and we were ready to take the plunge.

～

MAMMAW AND A HANDFUL of uncles helped us move. Thanks to them and Amy, we now had enough secondhand furniture to furnish the trailer from scratch. Only our beds, clothes, photo albums, a few trinkets, and the washer and dryer followed us from the old house. The furniture we'd been given was in good shape. All of it was downright attractive. Some of it matched, adding to the sense of newness in the home.

We were now a full half-hour away from Mammaw and the rest of the family. Although we were still in the city limits, streetlights were scarce in Karns, and farmland plentiful. Our trailer was at the very edge of the park's property, in a cul-de-sac, and a hundred feet from a train track.

"The lot rent's cheaper on this side of the park," said Mama, unpacking boxes as the sound of a train rattled the house.

"No big deal. We can just turn up the TV for a minute," I shouted back, not letting anything rain on my parade.

I was thrilled with my new room. The walls were ivory and spattered with a mauve and country blue design matching the rest of the trailer. My twin bed fit snuggly against one wall, and the cherry highboy Amy had gifted me sat along the other. Instead of using my bedside table as a nightstand, I used it as a vanity, plopping my purple Caboodles case on top. I even had a small closet, and enough room left over to put on headphones and dance in a circle, as long as I kept my movements contained. It was a dream come true.

I reminded myself to ask Sissy if I could borrow her new Debbie Gibson cassette tape to see how high I could kick my legs to "Electric Youth" without knocking into anything.

Sissy and Mom were working in the kitchen, finding homes for the pots and pans.

"Y'all wanna test out the dishwasher, just for fun?" Mama asked, tugging down the ivory-colored enamel door. She pulled out a rack and began stacking pans onto it.

I had forgotten about the dishwasher!

I was so happy for us. I was a reluctant dish washer at best. The feeling of soapy water mixing with food residue, especially soggy cereal, grossed me out. I knew that dishes were supposed to be clean after they were washed in the sink, but I never trusted the process, especially if I was the one doing the washing. Now, automated, sanitized comfort was at our fingertips.

"Heck, yes! Let's run the dishwasher!" I crowed cheerfully.

I crossed out of the kitchen and walked past the washer and dryer, setting a box on Mom's bed. Her bedroom was carpeted in mauve all the way up to the garden tub in the ensuite. Next to the tub and vanity was a small water closet that held a toilet and shelves for linen.

The water closet confounded me. The tiny room was not vented, so the temperature inside did not match the rest of the trailer. The lack of venting also meant that poop smell would have no place to escape except through the door that opened into the rest of the bedroom unless it soaked into our clean towels or the carpet that also ringed the toilet.

This was by far the most inelegant design of the whole trailer. It bordered on uncivility. I did not let my mind linger on what this indoor outhouse might smell like at the height of summer in the throes of heavy usage.

Any floral arrangement placed here would immediately wilt from insult. And although the resulting potpourri *would* make a delightful accent, it would be of little benefit on such a humid day.

Flustered, I shut the door on the commode and resumed thinking beautiful thoughts.

I walked back to the other end of the trailer, into the bathroom that Sissy and I were to share. Back at our old house, the shower hose had been broken for several days. I didn't like baths because I didn't like sitting in dirty water, so I had been squatting under the tub spigot and using it like a shower instead.

By that point, I was grimy from moving and from days of bathing like a street urchin. I couldn't wait to luxuriate in our brand-new shower.

"I'm gonna take a shower!" I yelled from one end of our rectangular homestead.

"Okay!" said Mom.

The water was fine. I took my time, using strawberry-scented shampoo to wash my long, thick hair.

Despite my love for ecological conservation, I planned to linger long after I was clean. Sadly, the combined usage of the dishwasher and the shower drained the hot water heater within a few minutes. I had a brief minute of lukewarm water as a warning, and then it ran cold. Icy cold.

I shut off the faucet and dried off as quickly as I could, taking a moment to admire the mauve bathroom curtains and matching pink shower curtain. Our trailer's color scheme was cohesive and *au courant*, reminding me of a dollhouse.

I couldn't believe we were really here. Suddenly, we were in a brand-new part of town; I had my own room, access to a pool, and none of our furniture was ugly. Plus, I wouldn't need a babysitter anymore.

These things were obviously no substitute for Daddy, but they helped.

I put on my oversized sleep shirt. It was white and printed with the Arkansas Razorbacks logo, a gift from Aunt Lola. I carefully rubbed some of Mom's Avon moisturizer into my cheeks, enjoying my ritual. I was sure that all the actresses on *Dallas* were thorough with their skin care, as well.

God was making it easier to look on the bright side.

I had to look on the bright side.

"What'd you think?" Mama called from the kitchen.

I could have said, *I miss Daddy* and *how am I going to make new friends* and *I ran out of hot water before I could barely rinse my hair*, but I didn't. God had done His part, so I needed to do mine.

"Refreshing," I said brightly, wrapping my wet head with a towel. "I really like our trailer, Mama."

"Me too, honey."

Back in my room, I got into bed and closed my eyes. Usually, I liked to read a library book before I went to sleep, but we had not yet visited the branch in our new neighborhood.

Instead, I said my prayers. Since I was starting afresh as a new person in a new house, I tried to craft them as perfectly as possible. I added more detail and flourish than ever before to say thank you, hoping that God would appreciate the effort.

Thank you, dearest Lord, for our new trailer, and for having money to buy it, and for giving us help to move all our stuff over here, and for our car, and please, wonderful Heavenly Father, help Mom find a job, and please tell Daddy hi, and thank you, Jesus, for animals and thank you the Holy Spirit or the Holy Ghost, whichever name you prefer, for saving endangered species.

Thinking of and praying for life's minutiae used the same amount of brain power as writing an essay. It was exhausting.

I got as far as *thank you for tree leaves and beautiful roses and even weeds, which I guess includes dandelions, Lord, but I think of them as regular flowers,* and then I fell asleep, safely repotted into my new life.

SWEATIN'

Mom, Sissy, and I sat in our booth at Shoney's. It was barely past noon on Sunday, but we had beaten most of the post-church crowd to lunch now that we were Methodists.

Unlike a typical Baptist preacher, our Methodist pastor kept the sermon short and sweet and without unnecessary verbal frippery or holy rolling that might clog the aisles and make it harder to leave. Our new church was a lot smaller, too. We didn't waste time waiting in the parking lot, stuck behind the fleet of minivans pasted with Jesus fish bumper stickers, just so we could turn out onto the street and go eat.

Church wasn't the only thing that changed. Mom had been hired at Karns High School as a lunchlady. The school paid better than the grocery store and allowed Mom to have some positive interaction with young minds even though she had decided not to return to teaching.

Sissy and I had also settled into our new schools. In South

Knoxville, I had attended sixth grade in a building that formerly housed a high school. The administration treated us accordingly, allowing five minutes of freedom between classes to go to the bathroom, go by our lockers, and still get to the other end of the building on time.

Karns Middle was different. Each student was assigned to a "suite," a group of four classrooms separated in the middle by squatty metal dividers, not walls. Changing classes felt babyish because our only movement was a single file, clockwise walk to the next room on our schedule. There was never enough room to stand in front of one's locker to gossip about cute guys or add another spritz of Rave to drooping bangs before social studies or math started.

Furthermore, the metal dividers did little to muffle sound from the other classrooms. Having to listen to four simultaneous lectures might have been some bohemian educator's idea of immersive learning, but to me, it felt like trying to study inside a giant fishbowl.

Still, the kids were mostly nice. Many of them seemed sheltered, although their naivety was benign. In some instances, their family's wealth kept them sheltered. In others, it was their lack of life experience.

The idea of losing a parent early in life was a far-removed possibility for most of them. They viewed me the same way they would a character in a book they could close when the story inside stopped making sense, at a distance and with a vague sense of pity.

Several kids were kind enough to offer sympathy, but they didn't ask many follow-up questions. I was labeled as *the new girl whose dad died* and left alone to exist. It wasn't so bad. My teachers liked me, and I made a handful of new friends who did want to get to know me, even with the stain of grief coloring my pages.

I liked our new church, too. The pastor's daughter and son-in-law taught most of the kids in one big Sunday School class. They were sweet and made it a point to pay attention to Sissy and me.

I had a crush on a blue-eyed boy at church. He was a year older than me, tall and brunette with a rounded haircut that emphasized his unruly, wiry hair. He didn't pay me any attention, but that didn't stop me from blushing furiously every time I saw him.

Even though I had a boyfriend in first grade and two of 'em in second grade, boys hadn't seemed interested in me since then. I feared it was due to my weight. I was the only fat person in our entire family. Statistically, this was quite a feat, considering Daddy had six brothers and sisters, and they all had kids.

I thought our family was good-looking, but I had no concept of my physical beauty beyond the size of my stretchy bike shorts. Fat wasn't beautiful or healthy, according to every magazine or gym teacher I'd ever seen. Well, every *female* gym teacher, that is. All my male gym teachers had skinny legs and potbellies that ranged in size from "extra helpings at dinner" to "third trimester."

Before Daddy died, a trip to Shoney's was reserved for only the most special occasions, like if we got our income tax return check or if Mama promised a magical troll her firstborn in exchange for the All-You-Care-To-Eat Soup and Salad Bar and a fried shrimp entree. It was rare.

Now, we found ourselves at the restaurant weekly, usually after church service. Since we got there before the Baptists and Presbyterians, we got our choice of sitting in either the smoking or non-smoking section. Although Mom smoked at home, we all thought it foolish to pay to eat in the section where the air was thick with others' bad habits. Plus, Sissy and I hated Mom's cigarettes. We wanted her to quit.

Healthier living was on my mind that day as we perused our menus. I preferred a hamburger, but I thought the fried fish sandwich with its thick slather of tartar sauce might have fewer calories. The sandwich did come with fries, but I was confident I'd have the willpower to only eat half of them, especially if I ate a salad beforehand.

The server took our order, and I hurried to the salad bar right after. I selected a chilled plate from the stack at the end and surveyed the choices. Never much of a salad eater, I skipped over the most colorful vegetables even as I admired them. The buckets of misted ripe cherry tomatoes and fresh green broccoli florets looked as though they had been freshly plucked from the garden. I preferred to appreciate them visually, however, on the buffet, not taking up room in my belly that could be saved for tastier items.

I loaded my plate with iceberg lettuce, then added a pinch of shredded carrots since carrots only tasted good to me when they weren't in chunks. Mushrooms were an easy pick because I loved mushrooms on pizza and thought they'd add some familiarity. I skipped the ham cubes, which were shiny with grease. I almost didn't add shredded cheese, but then I reconsidered and dusted the lettuce with a small sprinkle.

My favorite salad dressing was bleu cheese, without question. The ranch smelled too funky, Italian tasted like salty water, and I thought French was just ketchup and mayonnaise mixed.

Small plastic ladles inscribed with each name rested in the metal pots of dressing. I scooped up a ladleful of bleu cheese and tried to dribble it on my salad. Using a ladle to drizzle felt much fancier than dumping dressing from a plastic bottle. Unfortunately, the bleu cheese was much too thick for such a delicate approach. I was left with a big blob of chunky dressing right in the middle of my mushrooms.

I sailed past the bacon bits, feeling virtuous, and returned to my seat. I took a big bite of salad from the middle of my plate and decided to tell my family about a new fitness opportunity the principal had talked about at school.

"Hey, did you know -" I started, realizing at once I needed to finish chewing before I continued. The bite was cold and crunchy, and tart from the bleu cheese.

I liked eating healthy.

After I swallowed, I said, "St. Jude's is doing a walkathon. Our school is trying to raise money for it."

"How much does it cost to enter?" asked Mom.

"Nothing," I replied, sucking sweet tea through my straw. "You get pledges and the people who pledge promise to pay a certain amount of money, like a dollar, for each mile you walk."

"*Each* mile?" Mom questioned. "How many miles is this walkathon, anyway?"

"Um ... ten?"

"Ten miles? You want to try to walk ten miles, honey?"

It wasn't that Mama didn't have faith in me. She just wanted me to have realistic expectations about my athletic abilities. Before that moment, I hadn't shown any interest in physical activity. Years of Field Day ribbons with "Participant Only" stamped on them had made that clear.

Plus, I was a klutz. Even after years of church youth gatherings at the roller rink, I never got the hang of skating or proselytizing at the snack bar. Those were two prayers Jesus hadn't answered.

"I want to lose weight," I stated boldly, "and it's for a good cause."

"Well, if that's what you want to do, I'll walk with you. I bet we could hit up Mammaw for a pledge. And people at church, too."

"Really? You would really walk with me?"

"Why, sure. We could walk ten miles. Baby, I used to walk ten miles to school every day, uphill, in the snow."

"No, you didn't," I said, laughing.

Mama asked, "What about you, Sissy? Do you want to walk with us?"

Sissy, who was busy eating squares of fresh melon acquired from her own trip to the salad bar, nodded.

"Okay, I'll tell them at school," I said to Mom and Sissy.

We ate in companionable silence for a few more minutes, then Mom asked, "Are you girls about finished?"

I was still thinking about our decision as I hurriedly finished the rest of my fries. I was excited to participate in such a healthy family activity. I felt renewed hope that I might be as thin and beautiful as my cousins one day, after all.

Invigorated, I vowed to stick to my diet better than ever before. I planned to stroll around the trailer park every day to train for the walkathon.

But first, I needed to celebrate.

"Can I order some hot fudge cake?" I asked Mom.

～

THE FOLLOWING SUNDAY, WE were invited to lunch by Donna, Mom's friend from church. We decided to give Shoney's the week off to recover.

I liked going to Donna's house for lunch. She was a little older than Mom and had several adult children. All her kids, plus her grandkids, plus an elderly aunt, dropped by for the Sunday meal. Anyone was welcome, so long as they weren't bothered by the joyous cacophony of a dozen people all helping themselves to freshly baked biscuits and fried chicken at the same time.

Sissy and I plopped down on the carpet in front of the couch, holding our plates. Donna had a satellite dish, too, and she didn't mind if we scrolled through the hundred or so channels as we ate. The movie channels were our favorites since we rarely got out to the cineplex.

Flatliners was on, as usual. A movie about med school buddies killing and reviving each other on purpose wasn't the best choice for my impressionable pre-teen mind, but it played every Sunday we spent at Donna's. My biggest takeaway from the movie was that Julia Roberts had beautiful hair. I wished mine curled like hers, but the humidity in Tennessee was too strong and always left my waves hanging like ramen noodles spun in a centrifuge.

Lunch wound down, and Mom and Donna joined us in the living room.

"Did you girls get enough to eat?" asked Donna. Like every Southern mama, Donna's *raison d'etre* was to ensure a guest never left her table hungry.

"Yes, thank you," I said. "It was good." I had tried to restrain myself, but I couldn't resist extra biscuits and gravy with my chicken. I also managed to find room for a powdered donut, which was wedged somewhere north of my stomach. Why was dieting only easy when I was full?

Mom said, "Donna got that new Richard Simmons video. You wanna work out with us?"

The only thing I felt like doing with a bellyful of baked goods was taking a nap. I knew the walkathon loomed shortly, though, so I hopped up from the carpet and tried to be healthy once again.

"Sure," I said.

Sissy, who preferred Rollerblading, stayed seated. She scooted out of our way and pulled a V.C. Andrews book off the shelf above her head.

Donna slid "Sweatin' to the Oldies, Part 2" into the VCR. It whirred into action, and the tape started.

I knew who Richard Simmons was. He had been famous for years for his wacky persona, poofy hairdo, and tenderhearted views toward fitness. Formerly fat, he had vowed to treat overweight people with kindness and to use encouragement, not belittlement, to motivate people to slim down.

I had seen him on numerous talk shows over the years. Both his ebullience and his sparkly tank top and shorts combo were over-the-top yet inviting. His last video, *Sweatin' to the Oldies*, had been an enormous hit. Now there was a sequel.

Richard Simmons seemed genuinely interested in helping people get healthier, especially if they were people like me. I couldn't even outrun a slow-moving bus without a puff or two off my inhaler.

The workout opened with Richard sitting at a diner counter. After putting a quarter in the jukebox, he faced the camera.

"Let's sweat ... again!" he commanded cheerfully.

With that, we were moving.

Mom, Donna, and I swayed in unison to a song I knew from the oldies station. The cast of the video was then revealed. People with all sorts of different types of bodies were working out together. Pale-skinned, dark-skinned, women in their 30s, men in their 50s, slender people, fat people. They looked like they were having a great time. I was pleasantly surprised. If a lady who weighed a hundred more pounds than us could enjoy vigorous exercise, so could we.

Richard Simmons was an enthusiastic cheerleader, giving us heartfelt encouragement right from the start.

"Come on," he said, his doe-brown eyes softening in sympathy for those of us who didn't think we could last the whole workout. "I know you can do it!"

"We'll try, Richard," I told the TV.

The warmup ended and stretching began. Stretching was followed by several songs' worth of low-impact aerobics. Richard's choreography was thorough. We were stomping around so much I worried we might fall through the floor and into Donna's basement if we didn't pace ourselves.

I was running out of steam. I scaled back my movements to catch my breath. Mom, who couldn't keep a beat to save her life, had stopped trying to follow the dance moves altogether and was now just standing in place, raising and lowering her arms like the doors of a DeLorean.

"Whoo! I'm getting hot!" I said, fanning myself with the inside of my Bart Simpson t-shirt.

Richard Simmons was, too. Sweat glistened on his arms and legs as he grapevined his way over to the female singer, rolling his eyes flirtatiously as he wiggled.

Mama said, "He sure is cute in them short shorts."

Finally, the aerobic portion ended. It was time for toning. The crew grabbed colorful glass pop bottles to use as weights.

Mom and Donna didn't bother with weights, but I was refreshed and hoping to finish the video strong. Books would work! I picked a couple more V.C. Andrews hardbacks off the shelf above Sissy and got back in rhythm with the video.

My sweaty hands made sure the books slipped out of their jackets and onto the floor just a few reps into the song. No matter. We soon advanced to sit-ups.

The three of us stretched out on the floor. I didn't like sit-ups at all. They were the only exercise guaranteed to push out a poot, especially following a big lunch. My cheeks squeezed in embarrassment, aware they were being toned, too.

"Lord, ain't this video over yet?" asked Mom from across Donna.

The fibers of the thick, swirled carpet penetrated the back of my t-shirt and made me itch as I lowered my shoulders to the floor.

"That's what I want to know," I said, but I had faith in Richard and the other people in the video. If they could do it, I could do it.

"Girls, this is exactly how I looked when I was in labor with y'all," Mom said. She made a puffing sound with her mouth, similar to Lamaze. I paused my sit up and craned my neck around, glancing at Sissy with disgust. She returned the expression, just as grossed out as I was. Some of the more mechanical details of our births were better left to the imagination.

Finally, Richard began the cooldown. "This is for you," he said and applauded heartily.

"Thank you, Jesus," said Mom. "It's over."

"Cooling down is important, Mom," I told her, "Richard just said so."

"I'm gonna cool down on the couch," she said.

I was very proud of myself. I had exercised for a whole hour. I was feeling more confident about the walkathon.

After the cooldown, the members of the *Oldies* cast danced down a runway to mark the end of the video. While a cast member danced, their name and the number of pounds they lost flashed on the screen.

45, 20, 35, 110! By the third reveal, the four of us were clapping and whistling at the TV screen, celebrating with them.

134! 42! 65! 285!

"That Richard's an angel," Mom said. "God bless him for helping so many people."

Amen, I thought to myself. Under Richard Simmons' rhinestone tank top lay a heart of gold.

The last cast member, a tall, friendly-looking man, danced down to the end of the runway.

Seven hundred and four pounds displayed on the TV screen. We fell silent.

"Did that man really lose 704 pounds?" I asked incredulously.

The video ended with a freeze frame of the cast member, his arms raised in triumph.

We cheered loudly for him, happy for him, and proud of him. A hot tear spilled down my cheek and mixed with my sweat. The tear took me by surprise.

If he can do I, I can do it, I thought to myself once more. I hoped the man's life was now filled with the good health and happiness that likely escaped him when he was homebound. Thanks to his hard work and Richard's attention, he accomplished a great thing.

Considering a famous person a part of the family was dumb, but that's exactly how I felt after the video ended. I suddenly loved Richard Simmons with an affection reserved only for my favorite relatives. He was now my honorary uncle, whether he knew it or not.

~

LATER THAT EVENING, MOM and I sat in our living room, sharing sections of the *Knoxville News-Sentinel*. Mama and I both liked the *Parade* magazine insert and the funnies, but our favorite was the *Living* section. The *Living* section contained all the aspirational reminders of What Could Be, like the *People and Places* column that listed descriptions of Knoxville's fancy parties and the wedding section.

"'Mrs. Smith of Knoxville hosted an elegant spring baby

shower this week for her niece, Mrs. Smith-Barrett. The expectant mother will decorate the baby's nursery in shades of sage and country blue,'" read Mom. "Well, la-di-da. I hope the baby doesn't puke all over the new carpet."

I was too busy scrutinizing the pictures of the brides to reply.

"Her dress is so pretty!" I said longingly, gazing at a grainy photo of a blonde bride wearing a lace veil. Her dress dripped with sparkly doodads. The sleeves of her gown were so puffy the groom was off-center in the shot.

"After a honeymoon in Gatlinburg," I read, "Denise and Travis will return to Bucksnort, Tennessee. He is a garage-door installer for Sears. She is a secretary for Bucksnort City Schools and graduated from the University of Alabama. How romantic." I yearned for the day my wedding picture would be in the newspaper.

"Sure," said Mom, "it seems romantic now, but just wait. He won't make her happy."

"How do you know that?"

"Look how fancy her wedding dress is. He'll never make enough money for her tastes. How many garage doors can a man install in a week?"

I thought about it. "Well, she did almost push him out of his own wedding picture."

"Yep. Poor, poor Travis," said Mom.

I flipped to the next page, leaving Travis and Denise to their fate. I gasped loudly when I saw the advertisement.

"OH MY GOSH, MOM!" I hollered. "OHMYGOSHOH-MYGOSH!"

"For Pete's sake, Heather, what?"

"*RICHARD SIMMONS* is coming to Knoxville! He's going to be at a health expo at the convention center!"

"What? Are you serious?"

"*YES!* And it says he's gonna lead an exercise class, and anyone can attend!"

I was kooky with joy. It was fate. Just that day, I had grown to love Richard Simmons, and now I was going to be able to work out with him.

"Well, we've got to go, then," said Mom.

"Hey, Sissy!" I yelled down the hall. "Richard Simmons is coming to Knoxville, and we're gonna go see him!"

There was no answer, only the sounds of Top 40 radio coming from Sissy's room. She must not have heard us over the funky harmonies of Color Me Badd.

"When is it?" asked Mom.

I read the ad more carefully, and my joy deflated.

"Mama!" I cried. "The class is on the 16th. That's the day of the walkathon."

"Oh, honey, I'm sorry. Maybe we could go after we walk."

"Walking ten miles is gonna take me all day," I said sadly. "He'll be on an airplane by then."

An idea flitted through my mind, and I perked up. "What if we don't do the walkathon? We could just go see Richard instead."

"I don't know about that, Heather Pooh. You already promised you'd be there."

I sighed heavily. I had gotten a few pledges, too. Mammaw had pledged a whole $20.

"I know," I said.

I spoke aloud to God, casually, as if He was there reading the funnies with us.

"Okay, God, I'll do the right thing, but I sure wish you wouldn't have scheduled both these things at the same time."

God said nothing, as usual.

"I know you're disappointed, honey, but we'll have a good time at the walk," Mom said. "Think about the kids we're helping."

Mom was right. I had lived my whole life without working out with Richard Simmons until that day. I'd survive not being pressed into a room with a thousand other sweaty people, even if I missed out on seeing him in person. The enormous cloud of sit-up farts alone was reason enough to skip it.

"You're right. We made a promise to help the kids," I replied.

Mom tossed me half of the funnies, and we went back to reading.

～

I WOKE UP WITH butterflies in my stomach the morning of the walkathon, excited for the day. I tried to put an athletic outfit together. I selected a pair of leggings rather than shorts to prevent chafing and layered my faded teddy bear sweatshirt over a t-shirt.

I owned two pairs of shoes – thin white canvas lace-ups and the pair of bow-emblazoned black flats I wore to church. Sports apparel was as foreign to me as appetizers in Japan or dessert in Jakarta. My canvas shoes would have to do.

I slid my feet into my beefiest socks and tied a double knot in the dirty laces of my shoes. Lastly, I secured my thick hair in a ponytail so it would stay out of my face. It splayed wide, and I spritzed it with a pump of hairspray, trying to tame it.

"Mom! Is breakfast ready?" I hollered from my bedroom.

"Come and get you some eggs," she hollered back.

I took a plate from the kitchen cabinet and scooped some scrambled eggs onto it. I sat down next to Sissy and started eating.

"Can I have some toast, too?"

"It's in the oven," said Mom. "Now, be sure to eat plenty because they won't be handing out snacks while you walk, just water."

She handed me a banana. "And I want us all to take a banana, too."

"Where am I supposed to put a banana?"

"Stick it in the side of your britches, like a holster," she said.

I knew then we would be the weirdest walkers on the course that day. St. Jude's might even decide they didn't want us competing if we started pulling fruit out of our pants.

I didn't bother to argue, though. "Okay, Mom."

After breakfast, we piled into our Mercury Topaz and made our way downtown. We parked the car and hoofed over to the Clinch Avenue viaduct, the starting point of the walkathon.

March temperatures in East Tennessee were fickle, but this day was nice. It was cool – cold, really - but sunny. The temperature was forecast to hit 59 degrees. I would only need my sweatshirt for a few hours.

The three of us stood in line for a long time to register. By the time we checked in and received our official walker numbers, it was almost time to start.

"Come on!" I said, grabbing Mom and Sissy by their hands. "I want to be in the front. We'll get done faster that way."

"Well, I guess every little bit helps," said Mama drily.

We wove through the mass of people and made it to the front. The group there was unusually quiet. At first, I wasn't sure why. Then, I saw a local news camera.

"Shhh!" I said in a loud whisper. "They're interviewing someone for TV!"

Whoever was being interviewed was dressed like a walker. They were wearing running shoes, striped shorts, and a teal tank top that was stamped with *CELEBRATE KNOXVILLE*, the slogan for our city's bicentennial.

Wait. *Tank top?*

"MAMA!" I whispered excitedly. "It's *Richard Simmons.*"

"Oh, my God. Really?" she replied, forgetting to whisper.

I shushed her, and we listened to him being interviewed just a few feet in front of us. Richard reminded the TV audience that he was here in town to help them have fun while getting fit. And since the convention center was close by, he decided to pop by the walkathon to say hello.

"Helloooooo!" said Richard, interrupting his own interview to wave at the walkers.

"Hiiiiiii!" we yelled back.

I couldn't believe it. This was way better than any workout I might miss at the convention center. He was right in front of me!

I had never seen a celebrity up close before. Richard Simmons looked smoother and prettier than any human I'd ever seen. His hair was perfectly coiffed without a hint of frizz. His snow-white slouch socks, which poked out of his sleek sneakers like puffy clouds, accentuated his even tan.

He was shorter than I pictured, but somehow, it only added to his perfection. His cheeks were even kissed with rosiness, like a paper doll.

The interview ended. Richard took a moment to speak with the news anchor off-camera.

"He sure is cute in them short shorts," said Mama, again.

Suddenly, I felt Mom brush past me on my left side. She darted through the road closure barriers that were in place, holding the walkers back.

In slow motion, I watched her bounce her way over to Richard, opening her arms as if to hug him.

I grabbed Sissy's arm in shock. "What is she doing?" I cried.

"Richard! Richard! I love you!" squealed Mom.

Richard Simmons turned around and found himself face-to-face with my mother.

Please, God, I prayed quickly, *don't let Mom get arrested for accosting Richard Simmons.*

"I love you, too, honey!" Richard Simmons said exuberantly. He threw his arms around her, hugging her tight.

After a few seconds, he let go of Mom. She grinned goofily, frozen in place and dazed from his affection. By then, a representative of the walkathon was at her side, steering her away from Richard. She allowed herself to be escorted back to the line without comment.

"Did I just do that?" she asked us.

Sissy and I nodded vigorously.

"I'm just glad he didn't have you arrested," I said. "I guess he's used to having women run up to him like that. At least you didn't try to kiss him."

"I didn't think of it in time," she confessed.

Richard Simmons waved at us walkers once more before disappearing into the sedan that would take him back to the convention center. We waved back until his car was out of sight.

"He smelled so good," Mom said to no one in particular.

What an incredible start to the day! Now there was no way we wouldn't succeed. We had just been visited by the Patron Saint of Physical Activity. Praise God and pass the low-fat butter substitute.

"Are y'all ready to walk?" I said, keeping my eyes on the official walkathon timekeeper. He brought the megaphone up to his mouth.

"ON YOUR MARK, KNOXVILLE. GET SET. GO!"

I took a step, the first of 21,000 that day. I was filled with determination, thanks to Richard. I drank in the good feeling of my muscles moving and the sunlight caressing my face. I compared it to the standardized humiliation of gym class. If only all exercise felt this good, I might have fallen in love with movement years ago.

As I walked, I conceded a little, purposely quashing the

usual feelings of embarrassment over my size. Maybe all I needed to thrive was the liberty to move at my own pace and the encouragement to keep going, and the weight would take care of itself.

Or maybe it wouldn't. Either way, today, I would give my body the grace it deserved. This was the heart of Richard's message.

Mom, Sissy, and I kept pace as we made our way down Summit Hill.

"Hey, Mom," I said, "after the walk is over, can we go to Shoney's?"

"Yeah, we can go to Shoney's," said Mom.

"Yes!" I replied, mulling over the dessert menu in my mind. Perhaps this time, I would order the guiltless fruit instead of the decadent hot-fudge cake. I considered snacking on a plateful of grapes and orange wedges instead of a more traditional confection, and my nose wrinkled, unbidden.

I decided I would order a piece of strawberry pie instead.

Strawberries were fruit. I imagined sticking my fork through the flaky pastry and thick, sweet, jellied filling. The pie would taste like Heaven, indulgence and restriction in every bite.

It was a perfect compromise for me, the walkathon's most imperfect athlete.

BET YOUR BOTTOM DOLLAR

I had high hopes that after Daddy died and we moved to a decent place to live, I might have a shot at the middle-class lifestyle I'd always dreamed of. Turns out, it takes a lot more than lounging by the trailer park swimming pool drinking name-brand soda pop or a one-time shopping spree at JCPenney to transcend destitution.

I had been trying to emulate the "soft prep" fashion style since sixth grade. Now I was starting eighth. Most girls my age would have begun the school year with a fresh pair of tasteful canvas Keds and the kind of khaki shorts that only looked good if your thighs didn't touch. These shorts would be paired with braided leather belts and oversized t-shirts that casually repped recent vacation spots. Both the Hilton Head Beach Club and Disney World were popular choices, and both seemed equally fancy to me.

Having never gone on a vacation that didn't involve sleeping on relatives' saggy couches, I longed to move through adolescence wearing mass-produced t-shirts with the logos of any of these locations. All I wanted to do was look like everyone else.

In my wildest dreams, I chose a bolder and more cosmopolitan top than my less sophisticated contemporaries – one emblazoned with the Statue of Liberty. Although in my fantasy, my khaki-wrapped legs definitely touched in the middle (and then split off at the knees, like chubby river tributaries), I still pictured myself looping a small, color-blocked leather purse around my shoulder as I navigated the tourist traps of NYC.

These purses, available only at the mall, were also wildly popular but excruciatingly out of reach for me in real life. Slouchy socks in peach or teal (Why teal? No one looks good in teal!) and frosted drugstore lipstick completed my look.

At least my hair was somewhat fashionable that year. Back then, no one I'd ever encountered – whether at the beauty school or the "birthday splurge" strip-mall hair salon - had any idea how to cut my thick, curly hair. The best they could do was blunt cut the length below my chin and press a handful of mousse clumsily onto my scalp. The mousse added body to my 'do but also crunch, more crunch than dead November leaves, as was the style.

The haircut book at the beauty school had the audacity to

name this look the "Fresh 'n Sporty." There was nothing fresh about it except the fresh hell I felt trying to brush it out before bedtime. It was nearly impossible to get a comb through all that dried mousse.

The good news was that every hairdresser in town had also done the same thing to every pre-teen in town. Luckily, this triangular mass delusion helped me fit in a little better, at least until we went back-to-school shopping.

We had moved to Karns the year before. Mom had opened her first credit card account at the time - a JCPenney charge with a $500 limit. She told Sissy and me that we deserved better back-to-school clothing since we had just lost Daddy. She intended to give us a social leg-up since we were starting new schools.

A more likely explanation was that a bubbly salesperson simply convinced her to apply for one. Despite, or maybe because of, her hardscrabble Arkansan upbringing, Mom was susceptible to sweet talk, and she loved feeling adored.

She would become the most pliable person in the room if complimented. In turn, she would compliment the compli-menter, and the whole process might repeat. Eventually, the warm feelings and alternating words of affirmation would spin so charmingly, so dizzyingly fast, that if present, I would feel the need to sit down and breathe into a bag.

I suspect the saleslady implicated in this credit approval

transaction had no idea the turmoil she'd cause our family just by telling my mother, "Ooh! Your red hair is so *pretty*! Is it natural?"

In the hidden regions of my heart where unnamed longings and ugly feelings were buried, I wrestled with this fact. Could Mom have ever been sweet-talked by, say, traveling circus people and accidentally bartered Sissy and me in exchange for lifetime tickets to their shows? My gut said yes, and I couldn't help but eye every trapeze artist on TV with suspicion. Deep down, I knew I would always be one faux admiration away from forced rope walking.

In any event, that first shopping trip with the Penney's card was a previously unimagined paradise. I had never shopped for any type of clothing at the mall besides the orthopedic shoes I wore as a toddler. To my astonishment, Mom bought me the entire outfit modeled by the Junior Department mannequin.

My getup included a pink patterned short-sleeved collared shirt worn open, directly on top of *another* short-sleeved collared shirt, this one rust-colored, acid-washed denim jean shorts, and stacked pairs of hot pink and black socks.

The whole outfit resembled a rejected Saved by the Bell costume change, but what can I say? The year was 1990, and our collective rejoicing over the fall of the Berlin Wall was best captured in a swoon of sartorial capitalism. There were no limits to the number of collars or socks we would wear to celebrate freedom.

Unfortunately, it took less than a year to max out the card, leaving Mom stuck under a never-ending waterfall of compounding interest.

Last year's wacky shirts - my declaration of casual coolness to a group of unknown seventh graders - had faded, and the waistband of my denim jorts was now too tight. I knew that this year's back-to-school budget would look much more like East Germany's than West's.

In fact, Mom didn't mention back-to-school shopping at all. Sissy had already resigned herself to wearing her nicest t-shirt and an old pair of hand-me-down jams the first day.

Sissy did not yet possess my adolescent mouthiness.

"Mom," I asked the afternoon before the first day of school, "are we not going to get any back-to-school clothes *at all*? We're going to look so poor."

"We don't have any money," she said, and I knew that was that.

Mom wasn't too proud to call relatives and ask for cash, so I assumed she had already made the rounds on our behalf. Mom was a polarizing figure for Daddy's side of the family. None of them bothered to give her compliments unless they actually meant them, but on the flip side, no one usually bothered to give her money unless she asked for it and told them how she intended to spend it.

Sometimes she was successful. Other times, her temper got the best of her, and she would get mad at a relative for telling her no. Whether they had a good reason or not for refusing her (and, by extension, us), we expected to hear them be called "heifer" or "butthead" for a while until she cooled off.

Close to evening, Mom, Sissy, and I ended up at a dollar store near the house. We went in to buy some laundry detergent, which was a few cents cheaper than the supermarket. Depressingly, even the dollar store was celebrating back-to-school time.

Unlike teachers, lunchladies weren't paid during the summer. Mom's job at McDonald's paid less than the school. There just wasn't any extra money left after paying bills. Not even the leftover cheeseburgers Mom brought home after her shift made up for the long, broke summer.

I knew we'd get a few new clothes, eventually, when Mom got her first paycheck of the school year at the end of the week. But that was cold comfort to a 13-year-old who wanted nothing more than a pair of teal socks *right now* to match the graphics on a t-shirt that boasted the ocean adventures of Orlando, Fort Lauderdale, and, coming in 1992, Kissimmee.

I lingered by the $4 no-name canvas shoes displayed in a long row on a table in the middle of the store. No substitute for Keds, to be sure, but snowy white and attractive in their newness. Looking out the front window at the setting sun, I let out a big sigh.

I thought we had, at long last, escaped poverty once the Survivors' Benefits started rolling in. Sadly, Mom's financial illiteracy and our own hunger, created by years of lack, had caught up with us again. I was once again resigned to a long season of poverty through no fault of my own.

I needed a way to make my sentence more bearable.

Mom came over. "If I write a hot check," she said, "you can get yourself some shoes and stuff."

A "hot check" was our lingo for writing a check that wasn't *technically* backed up by enough money in the bank to be covered at present but would be within a few days. If the bank received the check and attempted to cash it before payday, it would, of course, bounce higher than a rubber ball.

Mom would also be charged a $25 'overdraft' fee if it bounced, so the gamble was real. If she had other outstanding checks and more than one bounced, it could cause a pile-up of fees and eat up a lot of money. If there were only two days to go before payday, no problem. The check might not even leave the business's cash bag for at least 24 hours. Writing a check on Sunday night and hoping it wouldn't be cashed until Friday, though? Not a safe bet. Only drunk tourists or down-on-their-luck divorced salesmen would take those odds.

Or maybe widowed moms. Gambling at the dollar store *did* sound like something that would be tearfully confessed in a 12-step meeting, but baby needed a new pair of shoes.

I threw my arms around her happily, grateful for her grift and almost as excited as if I had won a shopping spree at the mall. As befitting a low-level juvenile accomplice, my mind turned quickly to budgeting, calculating how much I could get away with buying without drawing too much attention to my happiness.

After all, only a person who couldn't afford the dollar store would be excited about shopping in the dollar store. I didn't want to arouse the suspicions of the underpaid clerk, lest her concentration be drawn away from the soap opera magazine she was surreptitiously reading while straightening her work area.

I leaned against the long table and pulled off my worn canvas shoe. It was molded perfectly to my foot after a year of wear and smelled perfectly putrid. I checked the size of my shoe against the selection in front of me and picked a new pair.

There was no way I was going to put my stinky pubescent *pied* in that glorious new shoe without a shower, so I hoped for the best with sizing and added the shoebox to our cart.

In the accessories section, I picked out a jeweled barrette that was too thin to hold all my hair. I didn't care. It was new. Even the poorly glued ends of the headband I chose, sure to poke excruciatingly into the back of my ear meat, seemed a defect worth accepting.

The dollar store didn't offer much clothing except for a few bathing suits and pairs of swim trunks left over from the summer season. I scanned the remaining pieces hanging on the circular rack, and my eyes found a red striped coverup on clearance for $8. I considered it – it wasn't even a t-shirt – but it had a hood and a drawstring around the hips, giving the blouse the appearance of something more expensive, at least in my eyes.

The thin coverup was the kind of jaunty nautical top one might wear on a boat ride or cruise if one's itinerary included a dirty manmade lake and a stop for cheap beer and diapers at the nearby convenience store. But still, it was new.

As I had done many times before, I pondered my lack of choices and vowed to make the best out of a bad situation. I tossed the top into our cart as freely as a woman reboarding from a shore excursion might toss her cigarette butt into the water.

The next morning, I walked to the school bus stop resplendent in my red striped coverup. I paired it with navy blue shorts and my bright white shoes. The Gulf War had ended months before, and I had not planned to look patriotic, but once again, I embraced it.

When it came right down to it, bouncing a check out

of desperation wasn't so bad. Mom hadn't done anything Congress hadn't done.

I boarded the school bus and let down the window next to my seat. My crunchy triangle hair waved gently in the breeze, reminiscent of the flag, reminiscent of the turbo air ventilation in a smoky casino full of gamblers. Buttressed by the fact that things had worked out in the end, I set my eyes on the road and looked forward to my first day of eighth grade.

WWGJD (WHAT WOULD GRUNGY JESUS DO)?

spent my entire freshman year pretending I didn't know my mother. I guess that wasn't unusual for a 14-year-old, but the difference between the average humiliated teenager and me was that Mom worked at my school as a lunchlady.

Lunchladies weren't considered cool. At best, lunchladies were faceless food dispensers, cranking out vats of creamed corn and endless trays of square pizza. Most often, though, they were low-hanging fruit, ripe for lazy jokes made at their expense.

Don't like the food? Blame the lunchlady, not the government contract with a corporate supplier.

Mad that vending machines aren't turned on during lunch break? Blame the lunchlady, not the school policy.

Grossed out because you have to bus your own tray and

scrape leftovers in the garbage? Blame the lunchlady, not your sense of entitlement.

Lunchladies were also not rich. You would think society would pay a living wage to the people who nourished their children and spent several hours each day roasting from the heat of the ovens and dishroom, but you'd be wrong. So wrong.

Lunchladies got no respect.

My own social standing was nascent and precarious as a freshman. Despite having nothing against my mother personally – except for maybe her deafening snoring that was audible even on the opposite side of our trailer - I couldn't take the risk I would be associated with her.

"Why don't you ever come back to the dishroom to say hi?" Mom asked me early in the school year.

"Umm ... I don't know," I waffled. "I guess I just never have enough time."

"Well, you need to. I've already told the girls all about you. They want to see your broccoli impression."

"You told them about Broccoli?!?" I asked, embarrassed. Broccoli was a character I had invented. She was somehow simultaneously a little girl and a piece of broccoli, and she lived on a farm with her human grandparents. Her best friends were a cow and a duck. Broccoli's voice was high-pitched, and the stories she told were dumb. She was not what I led with when meeting new people.

"Mom, please stop telling the other lunchladies about me," I pleaded, knowing I was asking the impossible. Mom was incapable of restraint when it came to bragging on her kids. Not that I would consider Broccoli a brag.

"Fine. I'll tell them about Sissy instead. She's getting so good at softball."

Luckily, Sissy was still in elementary school and far away from Mom's incessant boasting.

"Fine."

Mom soon caught on to what I was doing. She stopped asking me to come meet the other lunchladies and remained silent when my friends and I put our trays in the dishroom window for her to wash.

If this hurt her feelings, she never told me. She was easier to ignore the days she worked in the dishroom, but much harder to ignore when she worked the cafeteria line. I felt weird and uncomfortable pretending we'd never met as I handed back her own hard-earned money to purchase my lunch.

"You have a nice day, now, darlin'," she would say as she plopped change into my hand.

"You too," I'd reply in a rush. I knew I could never be a plainclothes cop. The guilt from pretending was agonizing.

By spring semester, some of my fear had abated. I had let my closest friends in on my secret, and with the opening of the new cafeteria pizza bistro, I didn't have to see Mom at all.

Not only did Mom never work the bistro, but the pizza was served on paper plates, eliminating the need for a trip to the dishroom. Now, I didn't have to worry about Mom popping out to say hi, like a gregarious jack-in-the-box.

At home, we relinquished our tenuous hold on the middle-class lifestyle. Even accounting for the Survivors' Benefits and Mom's job, unexpected expenses had a way of gobbling up any extra money. When Mom decided to move after Daddy's death, she didn't factor in things like vet bills for our pets, Cool Seal for the trailer roof, or expensive graphing calculators for math class. We just had to do the best we could.

I was mad at God for putting us right back where we started, money-wise. For the most part, I stopped talking to Him, saving my prayers for only the direst situations. I figured it probably didn't matter, as He never said anything to me, anyway. There were plenty of Christians, some even my age, who were adamant that they heard audibly from the Lord on a regular basis. They were enjoying all sorts of guidance I wasn't a party to.

Maybe it was simply because they concentrated harder during prayer. The TV preachers I'd seen receiving this divine revelation always had their faces pinched so tight they looked like raisins or toddlers straining with a bowel movement. I was afraid to bear down too vigorously in the service of the Lord. I was pretty sure that was what killed Elvis.

The school week was exhausting. I never had enough left over by Sunday morning to exert myself that way. I needed more sleep, whether it caused spiritual constipation or not. Mom released Sissy and me from the obligations of weekly church to rest, which suited me just fine. It felt more dishonest to sit in a pew pretending to worship God when I was this heartsore, anyway.

Our need to compromise spilled over into fashion. Financially, it was impossible to keep up with the latest trends, so Sissy and I decided to stop caring. We began to shop almost exclusively at a nearby thrift store, Smart Cents.

Flannel shirts were cheap and plentiful at Smart Cents. So were weird, clunky shoes, knit hats made by random grandmas, and plastic beaded necklaces, which were ugly but interesting. Sissy and I paired these staples with band t-shirts found at the Disc Exchange, Knoxville's premier stop for vinyl, tapes, CDs, and concert tickets.

The media called this trend "grunge," but we called it "What You Look Like When You Only Have Five Dollars to Buy an Outfit That Also Represents How the World Failed Your Generation."

Even though I had gotten pretty good at ignoring the Lord, I was still grateful He made grunge popular the same time we were living it.

Grunge began to work on me in other ways. Although I

was too doggedly optimistic to fully enjoy its bleakly poetic lyrics, I appreciated the genre's rejection of monolithic institutions and aimless wealth. There was a stark difference between us wanting to pay our utility bill with enough money left over for a new shirt or two and greasy politicians and preachers growing fat off exploitation and oppression.

From what I had read in the Bible, Jesus was all about turning institutions on their heads and renouncing those who made idols of power and money. That seemed wonderfully grungy to me.

I had fun picturing Jesus in red Chuck Taylors and a thrift-store grandma beanie. I liked to imagine him pulling the beanie down into place over his dark, wavy hair and then flipping the moneychangers' tables so dramatically the back of his flannel shirt poofed up like the sails on His disciples' boats.

Scripturally, God, Jesus, and the Holy Spirit were all different forms of the same deity. This was similar to how you could drink red Kool-Aid, eat it frozen, or let it soak into your hair as a temporary dye before a concert. I still liked Jesus best, though. Even when I was mad at God, I wasn't mad at Jesus. He made me want to be a better person.

I didn't lean too hard into trying to understand the intricacies of the Trinity. A lot of the debate seemed circular to me, like a never-ending desk chain of paperwork creatively assigned as punishment in hell. I just hoped my triune

Creator would cut me slack for only loving a third of Him wholeheartedly.

On our drive home from school one spring afternoon, Mom shared some news.

"Girls, I passed my safety certification!"

"That's great. What's a safety certification?" I inquired.

Mom made an impatient noise. "Don't you remember? Now that I'm certified in safety, I get a little raise. And then I can go on to take more classes if I want to be a manager."

"Cool. Are you going to try to be a manager?"

"I am, but it'll take me a while. Listen, there's gonna be an awards ceremony down at the World's Fair Park, and I want you girls to come with me. All the lunchladies in Knox County are invited."

"*All* the lunchladies? So, like a convention?" I asked.

"Sure!" she said. "They're gonna feed us, too."

"Who feeds lunchladies? Will they bus some more of y'all in from out of state?"

"No, they make you kids do it," Mom shot back.

The last thing I wanted was to be seen with a gaggle of lunchladies in broad daylight. Publicly acknowledging my mother's vocation was the same as broadcasting our Eternally Broke status, but I could tell it was important to Mom.

With Grungy Jesus in mind, I relented. "Okay, let's go to the lunchlady convention."

"You can invite some of your friends, too," Mom said.

I sighed. "They're all busy that night."

⌐

SURPRISINGLY, ONE OF MY friends accepted the invitation. On the way downtown, Davy's excitement over the weirdness of the whole event was obvious.

"I've never seen five hundred lunchladies before. What if they overthrow the city with their spatulas and march down the street in their white uniforms and climb on top of the City County building and try to overthrow the mayor?" he said. "That would be awesome."

Davy had a demented, though charming, way with words.

The awards ceremony and cold supper were being held in the outdoor amphitheater built for the 1982 World's Fair. We arrived to a flurry of activity. Lunchladies were everywhere, some talking and some setting up the supper line. There were also kids and other family members milling about.

"Aww, man!" said Davy, disappointed. "They're all wearing regular clothes."

"Maybe they'll change into their uniforms for the talent portion of the show," I said.

Mom flitted away from us and into a conversation with some lunchladies she knew.

"I guess we should find a seat," I said to Sissy and Davy. "Where do you want to sit?"

"Let's sit in the front," suggested Davy. "That way, your mom will be able to hear us when we cheer for her."

"You want to cheer for Mom?" I felt awkward not suggesting it myself. I was still coming to terms with being the daughter of a lunchlady. "That's sweet. Thanks."

"Sure thing. Plus, we'll be close enough to see them activate their lunchlady powers and morph into a giant lunchlady to fight evil."

Sissy and I nodded our understanding. Davy fit right in.

After some brief opening remarks and the Pledge of Allegiance (directed towards the small flag inserted into the podium), awards were given for several certifications. Those of us in the audience applauded politely after each round.

"Okay, your mom's next," said Davy. "Let's, like, stand up and run around in circles when they call her name."

"Are you crazy?" I answered. "We can cheer, but we are *not* leaving these seats."

Davy was unphased. "Okay, we'll just cheer loud, then."

Here we go, I thought to myself. *All these people are definitely going to know your mom's a lunchlady after this.*

The announcer called Mom's name, and the three of us erupted into a cheer fit for an after-the-buzzer shot.

Dozens of heads turned our way. We heard a few gentle laughs. Mom waved at us from the stage, clearly tickled.

A small sunbeam of happiness broke through my

embarrassment. Mom had taken the first step in advancing her new career. That was something to be proud of, regardless of how I felt about her in school.

After the ceremony, Davy bolted out of his seat to get in line for the buffet.

"They brought those peanut butter cookies from the cafeteria!" he exclaimed over his shoulder. "I've gotta get some before they're gone."

"Save some for the other two hundred people in line," I said to his retreating form.

Sissy and I found Mom, again talking to her lunchlady friends. She drew Sissy and I close to her.

"These are my girls," she told the lunchladies.

"Hi," I said, waving briefly.

I tugged Mom's certificate out of her hands to read it.

"Congratulations, Mom," I said.

"I heard you cheering. We all did," Mom said, gesturing to the lunchladies. She was obviously happy about it.

"Heather's the one at Karns with me."

The lunchladies made affirming noises, looking at me kindly.

"Yep, good ole Karns," I replied. I started to feel uncomfortable, knowing that I had been avoiding them for a whole year.

"Your mom is so proud of you," said a petite blond lunchlady.

"Uh ... well, we're proud of her."

Another lunchlady, this one with short reddish hair, asked, "Are you the one who does an impression of a piece of broccoli?"

Oh, Lord, I thought to myself. "Yeah, that's me," I said, staring at Mom, wide-eyed with teenage emotion. *I am dying of embarrassment,* I tried to tell her telepathically.

"Go on and do Broccoli for them, honey," said Mom brightly.

The pack of lunchladies leaned in towards me.

I imagined Grungy Jesus sitting in the second row of the amphitheater, His sandaled feet and mismatched argyle knee socks propped up on the back of a chair. He gave me a thumbs-up.

I sighed, and bit down on my lower lip, making my upper teeth protrude. I rolled my top lip back so it disappeared. Broccoli was here.

"Hi, my name is Broccoli." I kept my voice high-pitched and sweetly Southern. "My best friend, Bessie - she's a cow – told me that she loves yoga, except she calls it *yogurt.*" The lunchladies laughed politely.

"You know, because she's a cow," I said in my regular voice.

"That was right cute," one said.

I decided to make that the end of my set.

"Well, it was nice meeting y'all," I said. Sissy and I beat a hasty retreat.

By the time we made it through the buffet line and sat down, Davy was finishing up.

"These cookies are so good," he said with a mouthful. "I wonder if the lunchladies put, like, a potion in them to make you addicted, and then the potion turns you into a robot, so you'll help them take over the world and not know it?"

"Yeah, probably," I said, taking a bite of my own peanut butter cookie.

~

I FELT BETTER ABOUT things the next day. The lunchlady convention had shaken something loose inside me.

So we were poor. Lots of people were poor.

So Mom was gregarious and embarrassing and outspoken to a fault. So were half the people in Tennessee.

So Sissy and I stretched our style budget in a secondhand store. Kurt Cobain, the world's most grungy millionaire, looked like he slept in a bus terminal and took his wardrobe from the abandoned luggage cart.

I ate my pizza quickly during lunch and threw my paper plate in the trash. I decided to walk back into the area where the cafeteria line was. Mom was at one of the registers, ringing up a student. I caught her eye and waved. I walked toward her.

The student in front of me was tall with dark shaggy hair. His clothing was all black, his style more goth than grunge.

"Okay, baby, that will be $3.50," said Mom. The student opened his wallet and hesitated.

"I only have two dollars," he said quietly and put back an apple and banana into the large fruit bowl by the register. He had reduced his lunch by more than half.

By the way he said it, I could tell he was poor, too. He was trying hard not to draw attention to this fact. This wasn't some privileged jock, some king of the high schoolers, trying to pull one over on her.

Mom did not waver. "Baby, you put those back on your tray. I'll pay for them."

"Are you sure?" he asked quizzically.

"Yes. And get you one for later, too."

He put the fruit back on his tray and added an extra apple.

"Thank you."

"You're welcome, honey. You let me know if you need anything else," she said, patting his arm as he left the cafeteria.

When he was gone, she reached into her pocket and pulled out a handful of change. She counted out the remainder of what was owed and put it into the register.

"Mama, that was really sweet," I told her.

"Oh, it ain't anything. We're always throwing away food here. We've got plenty. I don't know why in the hell they charge you kids for it, anyway."

She made a good point. I hoped the goth guy had enough

to eat for supper since his mom wasn't a lunchlady.

At home, we often had cafeteria leftovers for supper. My favorite were the ham and cheese croissants and corn dogs. Sometimes Mom brought home Davy's favorite cookies, too.

"Being poor sucks," I said.

"It does, Pooh. But we'll be okay."

I hadn't just been talking about us.

"Do you do that a lot? Pay for kids?"

"We all do," said Mom.

"You and the other lunchladies, you mean?"

"Yes. We ain't gonna let anybody go hungry here."

The hot sliver of distress I felt made me squirm. The lunchladies turned out to be downright admirable.

I was too ashamed to offer apologies for ignoring her all year. Instead, I leaned over the metal tray line and hugged her.

"I've got to get to class. I'll see you at 3:30."

"Okay, Broccoli," Mom said in Broccoli's voice.

I walked out of the cafeteria, my mind searching for a way to try to make it up to her. Almost immediately, I walked back in.

"Hey, Mom. When we start back to school in the fall, would it be okay if I wore some of your lunchlady shirts?"

"You mean, like my food pyramid shirt? Why not?"

"Okay, thanks," I said, this time leaving for real.

I knew I would be going from one extreme to the other,

but I no longer wanted to risk hurting Mom's feelings in the matter. What was left to do now but loudly and proudly proclaim the awesomeness of lunchladies?

Although it was months away, I brainstormed an outfit for the first day of school. My black high-top Chucks and dip-dyed long silk skirt would look perfectly bizarre with Mom's t-shirt printed with cartoon drawings of dairy products. Sissy wore a plastic fork from an old playset on a cord around her neck. I could borrow it or just make my own after finishing a fast-food salad.

Sophomore year would be different. Next year, I would choose to let the light in so others could see more of me, more of us. I decided there was no shame in being conspicuous if your visibility helped others.

Mom was too valuable to stay hidden.

On my way to class, I walked past Grungy Jesus. He was standing outside of the rear entrance of the school, the door propped open, smoking.

"Good job," He said. He snuffed out the glowing end of the cigarette with his thumb and index finger and placed it neatly in the garbage can.

"Thanks, Jesus," I told Him. "I got there eventually."

"I wish you were here for real," I said to Him.

"I am. I like watching you figure it out on your own."

"Okay, but could we skip right to the season finale next

time, please? Personal development is excruciating."

"I'll meet you guys in the car," He said, changing the subject. "I love it when you bang on the roof when 'Floyd the Barber' is on."

"Floyd the Barber" was our favorite song off Nirvana's album, *Bleach*. Every time it played, Mom, Sissy, and I rolled down our windows and banged on the top of the car to the rhythm of the bass drum.

"By the way, try not to be so hard on God. We really love you, you know."

"Love you too," I told Him. Jesus leaned forward and kissed me on the forehead. He smelled like the vanilla stick incense I bought in the Old City.

I walked backwards down the hall, keeping Him in sight as I entered the classroom.

"Things are gonna be okay," He called after me, an amused note in His voice. "Grunge won't last forever."

"What comes after grunge?" I wanted to know. "Will we ever be rich?"

"You know I already talked about that. Something about a rich man and a camel and the eye of a needle?"

His gentle morality was exasperating. I made the *w* sign to Him as I disappeared into the classroom.

"*Whatever*, Jesus," I said as the door closed behind me.

At least for now, grunge was here to stay.

1987

1988

1991

1992

PÖR

Once upon a time, only a few short years ago, our trailer had been a thing of beauty. Our sweetly compact rooms showcased the best features of cheap suburban living – multiple bathrooms, indoor laundry, and an automatic dishwasher – all with matching curtains throughout. In those delightful early days, we had lived in a carefully crafted shoebox house made with love by a little girl for her dolly.

Now, we were living in a shoebox that might have once held a pair of expensive shoes but had been forgotten, crushed in a closet under the weight of unused hand weights and dusty tree ornaments.

I wasn't sure what had happened. Some of it was my fault, as I was loathe to do certain chores. No matter how bad a house was, it was better when it was clean. After the dishwasher broke, I couldn't bring myself to wash dishes because the feeling of touching the softened, left-over pieces of food in the water made me want to throw up. And it seemed pointless to vacuum because the dog and cat were constant, self-renewing repositories of hair. Pet hair was deposited on every surface, whether we had just cleaned or not.

I didn't mind laundry because I got to control the amount of fabric softener that went in the washing machine. The scent of "April Freshness" was one of our few name-brand luxuries. I glugged a large amount into every load, trying to offset the smell of the dog's corn chip feet and Mom's cigarettes.

Sissy helped with chores more than I did, but at the end of the day, house cleaning seemed like a losing battle. Mom wasn't especially bothered.

"As long as you're making good grades, I'm cool with it," she'd said. "If you want to live in a pigsty, that's up to you."

It wasn't so much a desire to live in a pigsty rather than a surrender into it. I was an all-or-nothing type of person. A day-long deep clean of a trailer our size would be wasted the second the cat used the litter box or Mom lit up a Basic 100.

On the other hand, no amount of cleaning could help what was happening in our bathrooms. The tub and shower insert in each bathroom was made of thin plastic, with inadequate foundation support underneath. Over time, with normal usage of the tubs and showers, vertical cracks formed in the middle.

As the cracks worsened, water began to flow into the

cracks instead of the drain. Eventually, the damage caused some of the subfloor underneath the tub to rot.

We knew what was happening. We just couldn't afford to fix it.

"Girls! Y'all need to be careful in the bathrooms!" Mom had told us as the rot got worse.

"We already know that," I said with exasperation. The toilet in my and Sissy's bathroom was now tilted, and the sheet vinyl felt spongy underfoot. When I had to go pee, I tried to feel for the floor joists with my feet, so I would be more supported. This was especially difficult in the middle of the night.

"One of us is gonna fall right through the floor of this cheap-ass trailer," grumbled Mom.

"When can we get it fixed?" I asked. "This is worse than having to go to the bathroom in the woods." I detested camping.

"Not anytime soon. I feel like I'm going to be paying off that bankruptcy forever."

Our list of debts seemed endless, but it really had only taken a few bills for Mom to get in over her head. She had two low-balance credit cards – one from JCPenney and one from Exxon – but it was still easy to drown in interest. Shopping at JCPenney was a distant memory by then. Mom was still paying off my school clothes from seventh grade.

The Exxon card was supposed to have been only for

emergencies, but that changed soon after the first swipe. Cold sodas and corn nuts from the gas station mart weren't especially nutritious, but they were a handy substitute for a real lunch in the summer when Mom wasn't bringing home leftovers from school. Soon, that card was charged to the limit, too.

Another cost Mom neglected to factor in after Daddy died was health insurance. Mom and Daddy made sure we'd been vaccinated and went to the doctor when we were sick, but those services had been free or paid off in cash over time. We'd never had health insurance. The school offered it, but Mom couldn't afford the premiums.

I'd been asthmatic since kindergarten, but the wild hormonal ride of adolescence (not to mention the pet hair and thick cigarette smoke) made my symptoms worse. We also owed a chunk of money to the doctor.

Mom had also splurged on a piano as soon as we moved in. She was very excited the day she signed the contract at the mall's music store. Unsurprisingly, it was to be paid off in installments until one of us hit it big.

"I bought it for you and Sissy to learn on. That way, you can follow in Daddy's musical footsteps if you want."

"But Daddy hated playing," I reminded her grouchily. Sometimes, my mouth was a runaway truck, like Mom's. "I hardly ever heard him play anything except sometimes at

Christmas. Oh, and one time he played *The Addams Family* theme song for me on that old melodica he found in Mammaw's basement."

"Then don't play it," she had said. "Just don't break the damn thing."

To be fair, Sissy spent hours picking out tunes and learning to play her clarinet sheet music on the piano. I never did. The only thing I figured out was the intro to Motley Crüe's "Home Sweet Home", in which I dramatically added an unnecessary damper pedal to every note.

Once I realized I was not a musical genius, I lost interest. The piano bench became a catch-all for my backpack and library books, and definitely not worth the investment, in my case.

But the worst repayment drain was the remaining balance on Daddy's funeral. Mom had paid the funeral home every month for over a year before she missed a payment. Then, she got back on track for a while until she missed again.

The funeral home started issuing ominous-sounding letters, threatening to take her to court if she didn't pay up.

Mama was furious. True, she had missed two payments, but it wasn't like she wasn't trying.

"Why don't they just dig up your daddy while they're at it?" she fumed. "They can prop him up on Woodlawn Pike and make him look like a hitchhiker."

"They charged too much for the funeral anyway. Right, Mom?" I tried to be contributory.

"That's right."

I knew Mom wasn't really upset about how much the funeral cost. She was upset that a company that proudly described itself as "family-owned" viewed her dead husband as a line item on a spreadsheet.

"If they had any decency at all, they'd just write off the rest and leave me alone. I've paid them enough. We buried your Daddy in the cheapest coffin they had."

"I remember," I said. I would always remember. The emotional laceration I felt over his death had mostly scabbed over, but it would never heal completely as long as we were still paying off his casket.

Somehow, Mom found out about bankruptcy. She went to visit an attorney who specialized in such matters. She filled me in after her appointment.

"There's two kinds of bankruptcies," she told me. "One is called Chapter 7. That means that all your debts get wiped out, and you don't have to pay anything back."

"But isn't bankruptcy bad?" I asked. "It is in Monopoly."

"Yes, it's bad."

"But you said you don't have to pay anything back."

"You don't, but it also ruins your credit for seven years. You can't buy a car or a house or get a credit card that whole time."

"What's the other kind? Chapter 4, where you're only ruined for four years?" I said sarcastically. Adulthood seemed rife with pitfalls. I didn't understand how I would ever afford to pay bills once I was grown. Rent, utilities, car, insurance, food, doctors, dentists, upkeep, and a new pair of shoes every now and then. Mom worked hard for every penny we had, and we had the Survivors' Benefits to boot. There still wasn't enough.

A future bankruptcy of my own seemed inevitable, written in the stars like a depressing horoscope.

"The other kind is called Chapter 13," said Mom. "They take all your bills and put them together. Then, you pay some of it off each month. Everyone you owe money to gets some of it each time you pay. It gets divided up by a person called a trustee."

"How is that really different from what you're already doing?"

"The monthly payment is lower," she explained, "and the credit cards will stop accruing interest."

"But what about your credit? How long does it take to pay it off?"

"A few years. And it hurts my credit, but not as badly as a Chapter 7 bankruptcy would."

"Will it fix things?"

"It will," Mom had said at the time, "but we'll have to be

careful with our spending." She sounded relieved to have a plan in place.

"At least I won't have to talk to those buttheads at the funeral home anymore. That's the trustee's job now," Mom added with satisfaction.

～2

MOM FILED FOR CHAPTER 13 bankruptcy, and life moved on. We did our best to pinch pennies, but pinching pennies if you're poor is different than slicing nickels if you're middle class.

Cutting back on restaurants and entertainment were ways for the middle class to save money. *Not having life-saving medicine* was one of ours.

I had been using albuterol inhalers for asthma attacks for years. The standard recommendation was that an asthmatic person should have more than a single inhaler at any given time in case one was accidentally lost or left at home. Too bad we could only ever afford one at a time.

On two occasions, I ran out of albuterol the day before payday. On both, I stayed up all night reading because I couldn't sleep comfortably without a deep puff of medicine.

If Mom had known, she would have pleaded, borrowed, concocted, or stolen medicine for me so I did not have to suffer in that way. I didn't tell her my inhaler was empty, though, because I thought I was simply doing my part to help. Mom had enough stress on her – we all did – that asking her to go find money twelve hours before we would be able to pay for the inhaler felt unnecessary.

Thankfully, there were no far-reaching effects from that gamble, but I would not recommend it as a long-term savings strategy.

Another way we cut down on spending was by delaying or outright ignoring necessary upkeep. It didn't matter if it was our trailer, our vehicle, or our hair and teeth. Maintenance cost money.

In addition to the warped bathrooms and broken dishwasher, the wooden decks leading out to the front and back porch had never been refreshed with a fresh coat of polyurethane. The decks, which began their underfoot service as sprightly tan planks, had faded to a soggy-looking dark gray.

In fact, if a bog witch ever drove through town looking for a spooky place to lay down roots, our trailer would have been the perfect choice.

Parked on the concrete pad outside the house was our 1987 Mercury Topaz. Our automobile's maintenance was performed on a strictly "as needed" basis. Mom mostly kept up the oil changes, but rotating the tires, changing the filters, or even filling up the windshield wiper fluid was left to chance.

The car was a money pit, anyway. Mom had already paid for a serious transmission and engine repair for the accursed thing because she couldn't qualify for a new car. The idea of dropping a match in the gas tank and watching the car burn to escape the inevitability of future repairs was tempting. But what else would one expect from a bunch of trailer-dwelling bog witches such as us?

Life was a money pit. Still, we were making it work. I tried my best to keep a good attitude, at least until the day the air conditioner stopped working.

Air conditioning was important in East Tennessee. Summers were humid and sticky. Even though we never had a/c until we moved into the trailer, it became a necessity. Trailers weren't insulated like regular homes, so they tended to retain heat in the summer and lose heat in the winter.

If only Thermos had manufactured trailers instead!

I was already uncomfortable when I went to turn on the air conditioner that day. I turned the switch on, used to hearing the whoosh of the system when it started.

Nothing happened. I turned the switch off, then on again. Nothing.

Frustrated, I twisted my long hair off my face and into a bun to cool my neck. The lower half of my bun, thickly poofy from a lack of trimming, threatened to unravel from the elastic as soon as I encased it. I felt it uncoil against the back of my head as if a squirrel were running around the base of a tree.

I squeezed my bun impatiently, irritation growing by the moment.

"Mom!" I yelled. "The air conditioning's not coming on!"

"Oh Lord," she said.

Mom stood in front of the thermostat, turning the air conditioner off and on. It didn't work for her, either.

"Well, shit, girls," she said. "I guess it's broken."

I plopped down on the couch next to the dog, sighing loudly.

A loud sigh of someone familiar with box fans.

"The air conditioner can't be broken!" I wailed. "It's not even summer yet. We'll die of heat stroke in here."

"Or we'll kill each other," said Mom matter-of-factly.

I was terribly sad about the state of the trailer. I could have handled the busted dishwasher by itself. I could have handled the lack of upkeep by itself. I could have even handled straddling the toilet in the dark by itself, but I could not handle all these things combined whilst living in a swampy tin box.

"Sissy, go get the fans out of my closet," Mom said.

She did as Mom asked and returned quickly, holding one in each hand. I took one from her and put it on top of an end table. There was no room for the lamp anymore. I set the lamp on the floor.

Sissy plugged up the other one in the kitchen and turned it on. I followed suit, turning the table fan's switch to high. Cat hair blew out of the fan and onto our dingy blue carpet.

I leaned over and spoke into the blades. "This succccccccccccccks."

"Things are gonna be okay, girls," said Mom. "These fans will cool things down pretty good."

I knew from earlier summers without air conditioning that fans never truly cooled down a house until after the sun set, especially if we were up moving around. There was nothing to do except sit perfectly still for the next several months with frozen peas wedged in our armpits or escape to places with working HVAC systems.

School would be ending soon, but I thanked God for the coolness of Mammaw's house and the library. The library! That reminded me.

"Mom, can I go to the library? I can drive if you don't want to go." My driver's license was brand-new, and I was intoxicated by the freedom of driving, provided we could afford gas. The library would be cool and quiet, a perfect place to spend the afternoon.

"I guess so but take your sister. I'll stay here with the animals."

"Do you want us to bring you back any books?"

"Yes. Something about the ice age."

Sissy and I drove to downtown Knoxville and headed into the library. The Lawson McGhee branch was the biggest in the city and our favorite. The entire bottom floor was for kids, the middle two for adults, and the top floor housed thousands of old magazines and newspaper microfiche.

I was ruddy from blasting both the heat and our Stevie Ray Vaughan cassette as I pulled open the heavy door. The car tended to overheat ever since the transmission had been replaced. The mechanic had instructed us to turn on the car heater when we saw the temperature gauge creep up. That meant any day above 70 degrees made the car interior feel like a camel ride across the windy plains of a desert.

My feeling of dishevelment disappeared as soon as I crossed the threshold. Even on the main floor, which contained the most patrons as well as the checkout stations, a cool and quiet peacefulness permeated throughout.

Sissy and I split up. I perused the new book section, choosing a Stephen King novel I had not yet read. Stephen King was my favorite writer. I found it refreshing to be scared by supernatural stories instead of the real-life terrors of not having enough money for the trailer payment or accidentally belching during my monologue in acting class.

When I was finished there, I climbed the spiral one-way staircase to the second floor. I had no need for the card catalog; I knew exactly where to go.

I adored the atmospheric heaviness of the stacks and the stale doughnut smell of the books. There was absolute silence in this section of the library. I went straight to 780.92, where the music biographies were shelved. I selected a Beatles bio I had already read a dozen times, its familiarity a comfort.

Next, I headed to 747, where I found Alexandra Stoddard's books on interior designs and personal style. I had been introduced via her monthly column in McCall's magazine, the one year Mom had been able to afford a subscription. I couldn't afford either interior design *or* personal style, but I found Alexandra's insistence on everyday beauty and ritual inspiring.

To mix things up, I wandered over to 817 and grabbed a couple of books from Lewis Grizzard. His views on feminism annoyed me so much that I couldn't make it through some of his chapters without wanting to flick him *hard,* right on the nose, in between his big glasses and mustache.

But I also couldn't make it through some of his chapters about his love for the South and his dog, Catfish, without bursting into tears over the sweetness of his storytelling. I loved him the same way I loved the relatives who embarrassed me with their opinions, taking the good with the bad.

My arms were full as I headed back downstairs, but I couldn't leave the library without a Miss Manners book, which was housed in 395. While Mom had taught us "please" and "thank you" and how to chew with our mouths closed, the finer points of etiquette bored her.

Miss Manners had gently instilled an abundance of guidance that I hoped to use someday. I knew the proper place setting for formal dinners and how to address envelopes if one spouse was a doctor and the other wasn't. My dreams of a more cultured future were still there, buried under the rotted bathroom floorboard.

The library building reminded me of the church sanctuaries of my childhood. Both were heavy with solemnity and surrounded by infinite stories that were holy with possibility. I loved them equally. The library was where I learned about the world while I was waiting to be a part of the world.

I remembered Mom at the last minute. Quickly, I grabbed a Jean Auel sequel from the spinning rack of paperbacks near the checkout. Were Neanderthals part of the ice age? I didn't know, but I knew they were set closer in time than any characters Danielle Steel had invented. I hesitated, not wanting to overextend my full arms, but then added a leopard-print Jackie Collins novel to the top of my stack. She had taught me even more than Miss Manners. I tucked it under my chin and carefully walked toward the checkout.

I left the library refreshed, ready to be distracted from the heat and poverty awaiting us back home. Back inside the trailer, the fans tried their best to keep up. Sissy and I curled up on separate ends of the couch with our library books, eager to enter other worlds.

～

As the months dragged by, Sissy and I began to decorate our

hallway, bathroom, and bedrooms with random pieces of nonsense. Anything, as long as it was weird and ugly, would get taped up or poorly hung by a single thumbtack. Mom didn't mind. She dismissed it as typical teenage silliness, but to Sissy and me, it had meaning.

An East Coast art critic might have looked at our hallway plastered with produce ads, caution tape, an outdated instructional pizza cutting poster from my job at Little Caesars, a t-shirt that said, "I'm Not Fat, I'm Just Fluffy," and a disco ball made from aluminum foil and understood that we were making a creative statement about not surrendering to the swirling forces that were trying to consume us, therefore empowering ourselves to reframe the situation to remark upon it in an exaggerated way, blah blah blah.

Then again, I didn't know a single East Coast art critic who had ever visited a trailer, especially one whose inhabitants would offer school cafeteria leftovers and generic cola as appetizers for a gallery opening. It was more realistic that the same critic would sprint full speed out of our trailer and off our ratty deck the second they realized they might sustain injury mid-pee if the joists didn't hold.

Before long, Sissy and I developed a defiant pride about our poverty. We were smart kids and funny ones, but no one was coming to rescue us. Whatever strength we had, we'd have to harness it to survive. Our resourcefulness amid this ludicrous season of life became a badge of honor.

Sissy called this state-of-being *pör*. We were indeed poor in the traditional sense, but the amended spelling and punk umlaut revolutionized the feeling surrounding it.

Poor was a defenseless orphan begging for food. *Pör* was a creative orphan dealing three-card monte on some days and being sustained by her garden on others.

We chose to be pör.

I walked out of my room one afternoon that sizzling summer. Sissy was standing in the hallway, writing on the back of an old poster. In big letters at the top, it read,

YOU MIGHT BE PÖR IF...

The sign paid homage to Jeff Foxworthy's newfound success. We knew plenty of rednecks, too.

Sissy began to fill up the blank space.

You might be pör if you consider Shoney's a fancy restaurant.

It was true. We did. You could get soup, salad, *and* fruit at the buffet bar.

You might be pör if you've ever had to pay for pizza or gas with pennies.

Counting out $5 worth of pennies with people in line behind us was not something I ever wanted to repeat.

You might be pör if the only reason you get junk food is that your mother brings it home from the school cafeteria.

At the end of the school year, Mom had been allowed to bring home some of the remaining bags of potato chips and candy that were sold next to the register. The sour cream and onion ones were my favorite. Sissy preferred the candy.

I was getting into the spirit of things. Once Sissy had finished with her examples, I added some of my own.

...something that costs $4.00 is "too expensive."

...you get abnormally excited the week before your family gets paid.

...you have to be picky about where you shop for groceries because you don't want to go to a place where you've written a bounced check.

OR -

You rejoice because this month, you've only had one bounced check, not six.

One month, six checks had bounced the week before Mom's payday. The fees had cost us over $200, all because we decided to take a chance on a full cart of groceries too soon. The bounced check at the grocery store had caused an avalanche of other bounced checks. Among the victims were the utility board, the phone company, and, worst of all, our church. The check for the offering had also bounced. Receiving that call from the church secretary had humiliated Mom.

Writing the Pör list was cathartic. Friends noticed it when they visited. Sissy and I allowed anyone to add to the list as long as what they added was true. Soon, the poster was full. We added a second. Lots of friends understood the struggle.

...you've made yourself homemade "pizza" with freezer-burned mozzarella and ketchup on a slice of bread.

...you've ever had to miss school because you didn't have enough gas money to get there.

...your family has a private pool, but it's impossible to swim in because of all the algae in it. In fact, it's more like a bio-dome than a pool because there are more frogs in there than there is water.

Pör attracted pör.

In general, Mom seemed unperturbed by our poverty. Although she loved a good fight and always saw herself as the underdog, she never focused her wildly jovial energy on any of our specific problems. Instead, the act of survival alone recharged her.

Sissy and I wanted proactive solutions like game plans, meal plans, and budget plans. We wanted to solve the problems so we wouldn't keep repeating them - if that was even possible - but Mom was content to merely batten down the hatches until it was all over. If we stayed at war forever, we'd never have to deal with the trauma and rumination that awaited so many soldiers back home.

Sometimes the pressure caught up with Mom, despite her best efforts to outrun it. One Tuesday evening, after a cheap supper of spaghetti, canned sauce, and saltines, Mom sat at the kitchen table, balancing her checkbook.

None of us had eaten our fill, but we were stretching our remaining pantry items to last the rest of the week. I found this heinously unfair. I didn't understand how I could still be fat despite feeling hungry all the time.

I remembered there was a box of generic orange gelatin left in the cabinet above the broken dishwasher. As I rooted around in the cabinet looking for it, Mom slammed the checkbook down on the table. The thin plastic checkbook cover made a slapping noise that sounded like someone's hand angrily popping the backside of a misbehaving child. I flinched.

"I'm sick and tired of this shit," she said angrily.

"What's the matter?" I asked.

"I work, and I struggle, and I still don't have a dollar to my name. Girls, it's gonna be a long week. We won't be able to buy any groceries until Friday."

Sissy and I were well acquainted with the pör grocery cycle: spend the three days before payday getting creative with whatever was in the pantry, go to Kroger on payday, fill the cart, and eat plentifully for a week.

Then, start the cycle all over again a few days into the next week when out of groceries. Supplement with trips to Mammaw's house for Sunday dinner, and hope a friend invites you to spend the night.

"Can't we just write a hot check and hope it doesn't bounce?" We had done this so often it felt normal.

"Heather, if it bounces, it's just gonna eat up my paycheck with overdraft fees again."

"Well," I asked, "what about calling Mammaw or somebody and asking for money?"

Mom said nothing, her shoulders slumping in defeat. "Because I don't want to hear another lecture about how I need to get it together and take better care of you girls."

Mammaw wasn't the only family member to offer unsolicited advice. "I get my check from Little Caesars on Friday, too," I said. "I can help then."

In the movies, a teenager's summer job paid for nights out with friends and designer sweaters. Real life was different.

I turned back to the cabinet and continued my search for the generic gelatin.

"Ah ha!" I said, "Here it is."

I grabbed a large, chipped bowl and dumped the powder into it.

"We can have this for dessert today and tomorrow. We've got cornmeal, so we can make some cornbread and pinto beans. I don't work again until Friday, but I bet Davy would bring us a pizza between now and then." Davy worked at Little Caesars, too. He was a great friend. Both of our households ate a lot of free pizza.

Mom said nothing.

"Mom? What do you think?"

"I think I can't take this anymore!" she screamed. "Tommy Joe, why did you leave me here to raise these girls by myself?" she yelled to the roof of the trailer.

Sissy and I looked at each other knowingly. Mom's heavenly laments were nothing new. Her most upsetting conversations with God and my dearly departed father occurred in the very early morning hours during the school week when she was the first one up in the house. There was no hiding grief in a trailer with paper-thin walls.

I bent to hug her, but she sat stiffly, not responding. To my dismay, she began to cry. Mom never cried.

"Girls, I hate this so bad. I will never understand why the Lord took your Daddy," she said.

I was very good at cleaning up messes that didn't include housework. It was another survival skill. My mind worked frantically, using every available carbohydrate from our spaghetti and saltine dinner to fuel my thoughts. I had to pull her out of this tailspin.

"Wait a second, Mom. Don't you usually round up all your checkbook entries to make the math easier?"

"Well...yes. It's faster that way, and it leaves a little cushion in case I mess up. So what?"

"Let me see your checkbook and the bank statement."

She didn't hand them to me right away. Her face wore a sour look, one that insisted her teenage daughter tread carefully in this matter.

I sat down at the table so I wouldn't tower over her as I did my calculations.

I worked quietly. Carefully, I compared each line item on her bank statement with the amount recorded in her checkbook. I subtracted the accurate cent amount from the round-up amount and wrote each difference down on a piece of notebook paper. When I was finished, I added the numbers together to get a total.

"Hey, Mom," I said at last. "We'll be okay this week."

"In what way?"

"We actually have $12.38 in the checking account. If we go to the ATM, we can get $10 out and buy a few groceries and still have money left. That way, we don't have to risk writing a check."

I kept my tone cheerful, trying to radiate hope. Sometimes, all I needed was a single reminder that things weren't as bad as they seemed. Maybe it would work for Mom, too.

"You sure about that?" she asked, a faint suspicion coloring her tone.

I tried not to take it personally. Mom's childhood had been full of deprivation, and she didn't trust easily unless awash with compliments. I lacked the energy to speak adoringly to her. Brief optimism would have to do the heavy lifting.

"Yes. Let me show you the math." I went through each entry, staying calm but upbeat.

By the time I was finished, she had relaxed a little.

"Can you girls buy some groceries tomorrow after you drop me off for work?" Mom's summer job that year was at a nearby motel, where she worked in housekeeping.

"Absolutely. We can get a bunch of stuff with ten dollars," I assured her.

"Things are gonna be okay, Mom." I stood up and hugged her from the side with half of my body, leaning my cheek on her coarse auburn hair. This time, she put her arm around my waist and hugged me back.

I needed a minute away. I took a library book from the perpetual stack on the piano bench and went outside on the front deck. Dusk was approaching, and the hypnotic ree-ah-ree of the jarflies enticed me to sit awhile.

I put together a shopping list in my head. Turkey bologna was 99 cents, and so were store-brand nacho chips. We could get a loaf of bread for 89 cents if it was on sale. A two-liter of generic ginger ale, my favorite, was less than a buck, too. We could buy all that and still have enough left over for a squirt of gasoline. That, plus what was in the cabinets, would hold us until Friday.

I opened my book on interior design to a chapter about dining rooms. The author believed that dining rooms painted in rich colors were elegant, especially with white trim. I filed thoughts of beautifully painted forest green walls far away into the future, waiting for the day our boat finally sailed past the choppy waters.

I hoped that day would hurry. Sissy and I were skilled crew, but Mom was still the captain. We had to keep each other afloat no matter what. I wondered how long I could paddle with one arm and still double as Mom's lifejacket, her lighthouse on the Pör Shore.

THE CHRISTMAS BEETS

It was senior year, and college was supposed to be on my mind. I didn't want to think about it. Instead, my days were consumed with friends and theatre class, and dramatic, unrequited teenage love. I applied myself just enough to keep Mom happy and retain my membership in the National Honor Society.

All you needed to be an NHS member at Karns was a 3.5 GPA, the recommendation of a teacher whose class you'd never fallen asleep in, and ten free hours per semester to devote to community service.

Since Karns was decidedly out in the sticks, the faculty sponsors kept the definition of "community service" flexible. We were a full half-hour from downtown, which, although in need of all sorts of help, was too far for the average high schooler to traverse alone.

I wasn't the average high schooler, having driven down-town and back dozens of times to visit Mammaw and the library. Even so, Mom didn't want to waste gas money on volunteer opportunities clear across the county.

"You can find something to do in Karns," she had assured me.

"What am I going to do here? Sweep the Food Lion parking lot? Help an old lady cross Oak Ridge Highway and not get hit by a pickup truck full of hay?"

I wanted to know. Karns was a nice enough place to live, but it was far too sleepy for my tastes. Any time I had a few bucks in my pocket, Sissy and I would make a beeline for downtown Knoxville. At Java, in the Old City, $3 would buy you a pot of Earl Grey tea with a bit of change left over to drop into the tip jar.

"Why don't you ask Dr. Jenny if you can help her?" asked Mom.

Dr. Jenny was our chiropractor. We couldn't afford car maintenance or name-brand groceries, but our spines were in great shape. Mom had gotten pulled in by Dr. Jenny's al-ternative health tractor-beam the year before at the Karns Community Fair. Mom was desperate for attention, and Dr. Jenny was desperate for patients, so it worked out.

I liked Dr. Jenny. She was nice and never commented on my weight, even though she must have thought it affected my vertebrae, especially when combined with my worn-out, hand-me-down Airwalk skate shoes, formerly owned by my cousin, Brayden.

Dr. Jenny's office was bright and friendly. She had convinced Mom that chiropractic was the solution to my asthma and Sissy's migraines. Her treatments didn't seem to make much difference for me, but the experience of being lowered down on the pneumatic adjusting table was fun.

Dr. Jenny had her weird aspects, too. She hung different colored crystals from her ears and neck, convinced they were doing something, and smelled vaguely antiseptic like she used mouthwash for perfume. Still, she was mostly normal.

"Yeah, I guess I could," I told Mom. "Do you want me to learn how to adjust you?"

"No thanks," said Mom, "but if you do a good job, maybe she'll give us some free treatment."

Securing a spot with Dr. Jenny for some of my community service hours had been painless. I straightened her office and designed a few bulletin boards. I also learned a little medical terminology, including the word *subluxation*. Subluxation was the formal term for a pinched nerve. I thought it would make a great band name.

I returned to Dr. Jenny's office the next month to volunteer more time, but I was still short two hours. There were only so many times I could sweep the patio or clear the office energy by clanging a stick against one of Dr. Jenny's tuning forks, especially if I had to keep a straight face while doing so.

Luckily, there were easy ways to earn the two remaining hours. One way was to bring in an old phone book to recycle. That counted as an hour. As far as volunteering went, it wasn't nearly as ecologically noble as cleaning up the banks of the Tennessee River, the way the NHS in South Knoxville was doing. However, it was still better than hoarding the old phone books in our houses, where each lay abandoned until November. They only ever regained their usefulness in our community briefly, serving as slick, makeshift booster seats for short children gathered 'round the holiday table.

NHS students could also earn an hour by donating a bag full of canned goods. The canned goods would be made into holiday baskets and given to the needy. This was a nice idea, in theory.

Over the years, our family had been the recipients of many philanthropic donations – from teachers, churches, the Lions' Club, and random groups of firemen.

My and Sissy's names had also dangled off more than one Angel Tree, including the time another kid with the same name almost walked away with Sissy's Barbie Soda Shoppe. The Soda Shoppe had been the toy of her dreams that year and the only thing she'd asked for.

Mom came to the rescue by pulling Sissy's gift out of the imposter's hands.

"Don't you worry, baby," she had told Sissy, handing her the correct gift. "Mama ain't gonna let that little girl have your soda fountain."

The little girl got the present she asked for, too. Eventually.

In seventh grade, some of my teachers pooled their money and bought Sissy and me new outfits for Christmas. My math teacher had delivered the gifts, leaving me utterly shocked by their kindness but also distressed. Being so visibly needy was mortifying, yet I returned to school after break with a huge affection for them all. The outfits were cute, too.

It was always embarrassing to receive charity, but personalized charity was less humiliating. I could tamp down the redness of my blush if I concentrated on the fact the donor had chosen something just for me. I could even maintain eye contact if I knew they chose it with love.

More than once, we received presents without knowing how we got on the list. Those gifts weren't personalized, only roughly sorted by gender and age. A representative of a non-profit or agency with altruistic ties would show up unexpectedly at our trailer and brightly introduce themselves. Most of them assumed we were stupid as well as poor and would substitute volume for vocabulary.

"DO YOU LIKE SCHOOL?" they would ask Sissy and

me loudly, trying to build generic rapport to go with their generic gifts.

"MOM MAKES US GO," I would reply if I wasn't feeling charitable.

After being handed a lighted globe or cheaply made teddy bear, Sissy would offer perfunctory thanks before disappearing into her bedroom. I would stay in the living room with Mom, effusively praising the Lodge Master (or whoever) for my mirrored compact and scarf set, neither of which I needed. Sometimes, they seemed to expect my praise.

While my heart was genuinely tender towards any person who spent money on a stranger, I loathed feeling indebted to them. Being someone's check-marked charity case was worse than being poor.

I considered my theatrical appreciation of their gifts payment in full.

As I had come to expect, the most loving attention was given to us by individuals, not institutions. I could name a dozen Christians who might drop off fifty bucks simply because "the Lord said you might need a blessing," but not a single megachurch that would keep us from getting hungry in the first place. Even worse, the fuller the pews, the easier it was to ignore the widow and orphans sitting in the back. The anonymity made it a breeze to abdicate their responsibility to people like us.

Still, they tried. They tried. I tried, too, to rise above the constant contempt I felt for the fancy churches, especially at Christmas. The Savior of Humanity was gushed out in a barn and placed in a feed trough where dirty animals ate. Did those churches really need all those giant red bows and handbells? Couldn't they help pay our light bill instead?

After the feelings of grief and self-pity came guilt. I loved Jesus but was a terrible disciple. I didn't want to be mad at Him or ungrateful. By most of the world's standards, we were pretty well off. There were plenty of families who were homeless, even in Knoxville. They weren't sleeping in heavenly peace.

But wait – why didn't Jesus help them, too? He was God, right? Why didn't He just help everyone? What was the point of all this suffering crap?

The gift I wanted most of all was another loving confidante to help me understand the divine. I missed Daddy the most at Christmastime.

I was grateful we had something to give to the NHS food drive. We probably wouldn't have if Mom's friend Ada hadn't already brought us a Thanksgiving basket donated by her small congregation.

Receiving food baskets was a lot like receiving other types of charity. If someone we knew was gifting us groceries, we might get a pile of name-brand items and a dessert as a little treat. Strangers, however, often used the opportunity to clean out their pantries, sharing any kind of corroded old, canned item they didn't want anymore.

How we loved to receive the expired and rusted items from these dusty cabinets! How fortunate we were to acquire their dented cans of generic green beans or ancient salmon, alms bestowed from royalty onto poor serfs!

That evening, there were only a few cans left in our cabinet. Sissy and I had made short work of the Thanksgiving basket, eating the best stuff right away. I figured I could get away with only donating about five cans and still having it count for a volunteer hour.

I put a can of carrots and one of corn in a plastic grocery bag. Two small cans of tuna substituted for a single larger can. The tuna helped the bag look fuller. I took the last can of Spaghetti-Os - that hurt - off the shelf. We had been given two, and I had already eaten one.

I loved Spaghetti-Os, but the sacrifice was necessary. Into the bag it went.

The only thing left was a can of beets shoved way in the back. *Ugh, beets*, I thought to myself.

Beets were disgusting. They smelled like sour dirt and had the mouthfeel of rotten apples. Mom swore she liked them, but Mom also drank buttermilk straight out of the carton. Her palate couldn't be trusted. This was probably the result of growing up on a farm in the days before the invention of pasteurization, or maybe a mule had accidentally kicked her in the head or something. Her brain couldn't comprehend what tasted good.

The can of beets had a folksy brand name and a white label, which was neatly torn down the middle. I wasn't fooled by its down-home marketing. Nobody made lasting country memories eating beets with their meemaws unless they were memorably puking them up in the back forty.

I placed it in the middle of the bag to shore it up, so the label wouldn't flop around and tear worse.

I remembered I needed to clue Mom in about my raid.

"Hey, Mom! I'm gonna take these cans to donate for the baskets at school," I yelled.

"That's fine," she yelled back. "I get paid on Friday."

Friday was still two days away, but we'd be okay. Friday was payday, but Mom would also be bringing home a lot of leftovers from the school cafeteria since it was the last day before holiday break. The cafeteria manager was happy to give away the food that would expire before January.

I hoped Mom would bring home some square cafeteria pizza. "See ya later, beets," I said, tying the bag in a knot.

~

I WENT TO THE NHS classroom the next day and added my bag of food quietly to the pile. My secret was safe; no one knew the real cost of our donated corn.

During English class, the teacher announced my name. Each senior that semester was to receive a short consultation with our guidance counselor regarding college. Today, it was my turn.

I was happy to get out of class. On my way to the office, I stopped at the soda machine, pushing all the buttons to see if a cold OK Soda would fall out on its own. OK Soda wasn't bad, but it wasn't good, either. It tasted slightly flat and indistinctively pumpkiny. Knoxville was a test market for the beverage, but it wasn't popular. Teenagers wanting to drink it only if the machine malfunctioned didn't bode well for the company's bottom line.

Nothing fell out, so I went into the office empty-handed and waited for the student in front of me to finish his interview.

Mrs. McClellan was my guidance counselor. She was tiny, with rounded, teased black hair that made her look like a lollipop. Her milk-white face was always thick with makeup. Bright streaks of magenta blush, heavy black eyeliner, and jazzy carmine lipstick adorned her face like a 1980s new-wave album cover. Grunge clearly did not interest her.

I couldn't tell if Mrs. McClellan was attractive or not. She seemed to *think* she was, at least, if her amount of cosmetic grooming was any indication. In addition to being a guidance counselor, I was pretty sure she was also a faculty booster for the cheerleading squad or some other club full of beautiful, popular people.

I didn't have anything against cheerleaders. In fact, my friend Shannon was the team captain, but I seriously doubted Mrs. McClellan and I had anything in common. I hadn't said more than two words to her during my entire high school career.

What advice could she possibly have to give me? I was too fat for the top of the pyramid?

"Are you Heather?" she said, looking down at her paper.

"That's me," I replied.

"Come into my office," Mrs. McClellan said with a sharp East Tennessee accent even twangier than mine, if that were possible.

She started complaining right away, I guess to make small talk.

"I've got so many seniors to see and not enough time," she told me, moving a stack of papers from one side of her desk to the other. She sounded like an angry banjo.

"I'm sorry about that," I answered politely. I wasn't sure what else to say.

"Well..." she said and trailed off. "Now let's see. Heather. Are you thinking of going to college?" She again bent her bubble-shaped head to the paper in her hand, reading my educational statistics. I didn't say anything.

"Your grades are good. Very good."

I couldn't see her expression because of the size of her hairdo, but she sounded impressed.

"Right now, you're ranked eighth in the class."

I could have been ranked higher, but what was the point of working harder but not being able to afford my dream college? Even if I ended up with enough grants and scholarships for tuition and books, I couldn't afford room and board. Or winter clothes. Or club fees. Or new lipsticks for dates. There was no point in dreaming of a New England collegiate experience.

Dreaming was painful. I told myself that my sensible outlook on the matter was just as good as weekend getaways to Manhattan or all-night study seshes with new blue-blooded friends.

Apparently, there were people who put themselves through college by working multiple jobs, going to class, and still finding time to crochet booties for hospital preemies in need.

I could never be one of these never-sleeping psychopaths. Full-time school and a part-time job barely allowed me to finish my homework and participate in the most ridiculous of all extra-curricular activities, high school theatre.

"I've applied to UT," I told her. The University of Tennessee was right in the heart of downtown Knoxville. I could attend class, party until I puked, and still make it home in time to hear the 3 am train rattle the trailer as I drifted off to sleep. Yippee.

"Well, UT is certainly not a bad school at all. Not at all," said Mrs. McClellan. Her voice carried a slight note of confusion. "Are you a big Vols fan?"

Oh, definitely, I thought to myself. *Our family has our own skybox, and we haven't missed a game in two generations!*

"Sure am!" I said with a big grin.

Mrs. McClellan looked at me through narrowed eyes. Suddenly, she had an epiphany.

"Doesn't your mom work in the cafeteria?"

"Uh… yeah."

"I knew you looked familiar," she said.

I smiled. At least she had a clue now how to help.

"So," she said, again quickly glancing down at my name, "Heather. I'm sure UT would be happy to have you. You're a good student. When you get accepted, come back to my office, and I'll make sure you get a FAFSA application."

"What's that?" I worked through the acronym in my mind. Free Aid for Students Applying? Fat Ass Female Seeks Approval?

"It's the application for college financial aid to see how many grants and loans you qualify for," she said.

Loans? We couldn't afford bones.

Mrs. McClellan stood up. Our interview was over. I did not feel counseled in the slightest. To be fair, I did feel guided as she guided me out of her office.

There was another girl waiting to be seen. We had been in the same Biology II class last year, so I gave her a half-hearted teenage wave. She acknowledged me with a half-smile.

I turned to say bye to Mrs. McClellan.

"Have a good day," I said at the same time she announced the next student's name.

She hadn't heard me. I left the office and shut the door behind me.

"Thanks for nothing, sucker head," I said to the empty hallway. It made me feel a little better.

～

AFTER SCHOOL WAS OVER on Friday, I climbed into the car with Mom.

"I'm sooooo glad we're on break now," I told her. "Almost three weeks of freedom." All this and payday, too. "Can we rent some videos tonight?"

"Sure," Mom said.

"What kind of cafeteria leftovers did they give you?"

"Oh, I got all sorts of stuff in the trunk."

"Did you get any of those French bread pizzas?" Those were even better than the square kind with sausage. The French ones were simple loaves smothered in butter and cheese. I loved to dip them in spaghetti sauce.

"Yeah, I think so."

"Yay."

"How was school?"

"Pretty good. I forgot to tell you about my appointment with Mrs. McClellan the other day," I said.

"What did Mrs. McClellan have to say about the world?"

"She asked me if I was attending college. And she told me to come by her office to get a financial aid form when I was accepted. I spent more time walking down to her office than actually talking to her."

"You still gonna apply at UT?" asked Mom.

"Yeah. I mean, it's not like we can afford anything else."

"Well, if you find a place you really want to attend, you should apply."

Mom said this because it was what she was supposed to say. We both knew the truth, though. If she left it up to me, I'd never look for anything else.

For all her dogged bluster, Mom wasn't especially interested in helping me secure funding for an expensive education. There was no thrill of survival in that sacrifice. A college degree was the same to her no matter where I earned it.

"I wouldn't even know where to start," I lied. "I don't even know what I'm going to major in."

"You could get your teaching certificate, like me," she said.

"And never use it, like you?" I reminded her. "No thanks. Kids are the worst."

"What about communications? Or French? You're good at French."

"*Je suis* not good enough at French to major in it." I actually was good at French, having mastered five semesters of it, but as usual, I lacked faith. And confidence. And francs. "How would I ever afford to visit Paris to practice all those subjunctive verb tenses in person?"

I knew I was smart. I knew I wanted to go from poor to rich or at least have enough money one day to buy a house and go on vacation occasionally. I had no idea, though, how to read the map to get there. I only wanted to go to college in the hope that someone would teach me how. I wanted to learn new things in new places.

Since kindergarten, Mom had hammered into Sissy and me how important college was. She had been the first person in her family to graduate. Now that it was here, she didn't have much advice.

"Well, what do you want to do? What could you see yourself doing after college?" Mom asked.

What I wanted to do was feel safe, to shift the burden of existing hand-to-mouth to someone else for a while, so I could sit silently with myself and start processing all this trauma.

But Mom couldn't help me with that. She couldn't help herself with that, either.

I clung to the activity that brought me the most joy and

adulation in high school. "The only thing I really want to do is act, I guess."

Acting was easy. I was used to pretending, anyway, and my sensitive nature allowed me burst into tears at the drop of a hat. There didn't seem much to acting besides that. On the other hand, while the sound of applause stirred me, so did any positive interaction with others. Maybe I just needed attention.

"I guess," I repeated.

"You should major in Theatre, then," said Mom. "You already lettered in it." Most kids who lettered did so in sports. Not me.

I tried to picture myself on the stage of the Clarence Brown Theatre. Had they ever had a plus-size Ophelia? Definitely not, but there would be plenty of time to slim down if I decided to audition as a junior or senior. I doubted freshmen got cast in any roles at all.

"That's true, and I would have to take a bunch of core classes, anyway. It's not like I wouldn't haven't a few semesters to make up my mind."

"Well, see there?" Mom said, "that wasn't so hard, was it?"

The decision about my future had been made so casually.

"Heather Pooh," Mom said, "you should major in whatever makes you happy. I just want you to be happy." She patted my leg with affection.

A heavy cloak of sadness enveloped me. Mom's gift of freedom had a high cost. *Do what makes you happy*, the pat said. *I'll support you no matter what but figure it out on your own. I did.* My grandfather had kicked Mom out of his house when she announced she was going to college. She left him behind to get her degree.

Mom would never do that to me, so I already had it easier. That was her gift. The absence of parental absence.

You'll be fine, the pat said.

We got home, and I helped unload the trunk. There was a bounty of wrapped frozen pizza slices divided by paper liners, individual bags of chips, fruit, and huge logs of unsliced potato candy. Mom and I made trip after trip from the car to the fridge.

After the top layer of cafeteria food was removed from the trunk, I noticed a cardboard box full of cans.

"Hey, Mom!" I shouted. "Who gave us this?"

"Somebody at school. They put us on a poor people list. One of the teachers handed it to me and told me Merry Christmas."

I felt a dusting of embarrassment. Compared to the blizzard of humiliation from my time with Mrs. McClellan, though, these were gentle flurries that wouldn't have even knocked Santa off his sled.

"Yay for us," I said. Hopefully, there was good stuff inside.

I thought I saw the outline of a package of pudding. Pudding was good. Comforting.

I hoisted the box out of the trunk and brought it inside. I put it on the kitchen table to unpack.

I was still thinking about my appointment with Mrs. McClellan. "Hey, Mom, would you help me fill out that financial aid form when we get it? I'm gonna need help with, like, tax info and stuff."

Mom was busy rearranging the fridge to make room for all the pizza. "I'll help, Heather, but your guidance counselor can help, too." She sounded impatient. "Don't be afraid of Mrs. McClellan. She puts her drawers on one leg at a time like everybody else."

"I'm not afraid of her," I said. "I just don't like her. I've been at Karns for four years and I was counseled for a grand total of five minutes. It's not my fault she's overworked."

"The world is full of people we don't like," said Mom, closing the door to the fridge and going into her bedroom to change out of her work clothes.

I knew the world was full of people I didn't like and who didn't like me. The world was also full of people who looked down on us, through us, and over us, only noticing us when it was time to donate their dusty cans of Dinty Moore. I didn't need exposure to them; I needed protection from them.

Why couldn't she just say yes? I loved Mom, but tough

skin and scar tissue were not the same. Why did she think birds had to be shoved so hard out of the nest? I was already weary from years of parenting myself, and anyway, my nest had been set on fire the minute Daddy died. A baby bird with a broken wing couldn't fly far.

Angrily, I began to unpack the box, placing the cans on the kitchen table harder than necessary. At least there was a lot of variety in our holiday provision. The small square package I spied in the trunk *was* pudding. The food pantry staples were also there – corn, peas, green beans – along with a packet of powdered gravy, peanut butter, ravioli, a container of stuffing, and some flavored rice.

My anger began to melt. This was the nicest donated box we'd received in a long time. We'd be able to use all of this. Plus, we had all the food from the cafeteria. I relaxed a little.

A bit of holiday cheer returned to my heart. I said a hasty prayer of thanks in my head that wasn't even sarcastic. Maybe I was being too hard on Mom. She had been traumatized, too, and was probably doing the best she could.

After a moment's pause, I chose to think the best about Mrs. McClellan as well. She was probably worn out and underpaid like every other public school employee in Tennessee. I took a deep breath and tried to picture doing something nice with her, like picking out a nail polish color together for matching pedicures. I bet she'd even let me choose the color.

On second thought, UT wasn't a bad school. Knoxville wasn't a bad place.

I reached back into the box to grab another can. Conceivably, I could learn everything I needed to know without having to trudge through a single blustery New England winter. Perhaps I would have wonderful professors at UT who -

I felt something touch my hand. Startled, I leaned forward to see what it was.

The down-home can of beets with the white label torn neatly down the middle, despised by all except the beet farm's corporate shareholders and my mother, donated hotly and hastily from this house several days ago, had reappeared. Its floppy label had brushed me gently, like a kitten's paw requesting a toy.

"Are you serious?" I asked the beets.

I picked up the can in disgust. As if on cue, I heard the mournful sound of a train whistle in the distance, adding its lament to mine.

You can never escape this life, Heather, the beets whispered. *You are too poor to leave home, and you always will be. And even if you break free, you will be captured and returned to this trailer. Why, just look at me!*

Fury filled my chest, warming me and turning my cheeks red. As the train slid down the tracks close to our thin metal house, the walls began to shake as usual.

The beets weren't finished. *You think it's hard now? Wait until you're thirty-five and unmarried and still living with your mother. After all, the world's a scary place! And expensive, too. I'm sure you'll both look great in your matching threadbare mock turtlenecks and embroidered vests!*

The train was now speeding past our trailer. The whooshing sounds of heavy clanking cars and the metallic zing of wheels kissing rails filled every corner. I tightened my grip on the can of beets, covering its mouth and drowning out its incessant mockery. I walked two steps to the garbage can. I hurled the beets into the trash with all the strength in my arm.

"I don't think so," I said aloud.

"What?" yelled Mom from her bedroom. "Did you say something?"

The deafening sound of the train finally began to fade. I exhaled, happy to hear myself think again.

I'd won. For now. After I had broken down the cardboard box, I twisted the thick folds into the wastebasket, unable to resist a parting shot.

"If you ever say that to me again," I said, loud enough for my voice to carry to the bottom of the garbage can, "I will yank your entire family from the ground and feed you to starving meemaws."

The hateful canned vegetable stayed quiet, buried in the trash where it belonged.

LUNCHLADIES BOUGHT MY PROM DRESS

"If you don't go to the prom with me, I will die of embarrassment," I told Davy emphatically in the spring of 1996. "Please, please do not make me be the fat girl who goes to prom alone."

"Okay, fine!" my best friend said. "Geez, I was going to ask you anyway."

"Oh, thank God," I said and breathed a sigh of relief.

I didn't have a boyfriend, and he didn't have a girlfriend. Even though Davy dated plenty, he happened to be single and ready to mingle during the last semester of high school. My romantic endeavors were far fewer in quantity but infinitely more melodramatic. It was good I was single my entire senior year; no teenage boy was built sturdy enough to endure my irradiated dysfunctional devotion or perpetually tear-stained face.

Going to prom with Davy was not a consolation prize. He was cute, funny, and a good student. We had been friends for several years and spent countless hours at each other's houses. He was part of the family. I could absolutely be myself around him. I felt comfortable telling him anything.

"I need to sign off on your tuxedo. I don't want us to look bad."

He stared at me with eyes wide, annoyed. "I know how to pick out a tuxedo! We just have to match my vest to your dress color."

Davy collected patterned sweaters and khaki pants from Structure, the preppy guys' store at the mall, and was the type who woke up early to style his hair. He always looked pulled together.

I relented. "Sorry. I know you know how to dress. I'm just nervous."

"You can go with me to pick out a tuxedo. I don't mind. What kind of dress are you going to get?"

"I don't know," I said sarcastically. "A cheap one? It just depends on how much Mom will let me spend. Then, I have to find one and buy it before we spend all our money on, like, the trailer payment and food."

Davy nodded in understanding. His family was poor, too. They had only recently moved into a rental house after living in a housing project for years. Their family had been financially obliterated after his mom and stepdad had divorced. He understood the grind.

"You wanna go to the mall and look around? I'll drive."

That was another great thing about Davy. If he had money, I had money. He always shared.

"Yeah, why not? Maybe we'll get lucky."

We climbed into his white Nissan Sentra – which would be his in only 59 more payments – and headed over to East Towne Mall.

There were two malls in Knoxville, West Town and East Towne, which was spelled with an "e" to trick shoppers into thinking it was fancy. It wasn't. East Towne was a clean, serviceable, standard shopping mall with two stories and a food court. West Town, however, was far more popular. With popularity came higher prices.

"Where do you want to go first?" Davy asked.

"I dunno. What kind of tuxedo do you want to get? Please don't get the kind with a colored cummerbund. You'll look like a party dude from, like, ten years ago."

"I think I'm going to get a vest instead. And maybe one of those shirts with the single button instead of a bowtie."

The mandarin collar was the latest trend, and Davy was well-styled. He'd look great in that choice. There was only one problem.

"Okay, but if you go with something trendy, be aware that

people who see your prom picture in the future will instantly know the year you graduated high school."

"I'm always gonna look cool," he said jokingly, rubbing his hand over his Caesar cut. Most of our theatre class watched *E.R.* We all either wanted to look like George Clooney or date him. Or both.

"Of that, I have no doubt," I said, linking arms with him and steering him into Proffitt's, the local department store.

I considered Proffitt's a place for browsing, not buying. I had never owned a single thing from the store in my life. *Businesspeople* shopped here.

As Davy and me made our way to the dresses, I thought about what it would feel like to buy one of their suits. How wonderful would it be to pick out a coordinating scarf or pocket square to wear to a job at an accounting firm or bank? What would it feel like to wear that expensive outfit sitting in a glass office?

"Tell McCormick he's done!" I pictured myself barking into the phone. "I'll have to save this account myself. Luckily, I'm wearing my single-breasted Tommy Hilfiger blazer and sensible leather pumps. Meet me for a celebration scotch in twenty."

My eyes feasted on the colorful cosmetics bays as we walked by. Spring-green signs announced Clinique bonus time.

"I wish I had the money for a makeover," I told Davy. "I'd have an entire closet full of makeup if I could."

"Why do girls need all that junk?" he said. "You're pretty without it. Too much makeup makes y'all look like Dr. Frank-N-Furter."

I pretended to be offended. "And not enough makeup makes us look like Riff Raff."

"Well, dammit...Janet," Davy said, and we both snickered.

The prom dress display at Proffitt's was a disappointment. Shimmering columns of color filled the entire corner of the store but in a mostly subdued palette. We were surrounded by plum, black, burgundy, and hunter green. Where were the paillettes and bright fuchsia rickrack?

Out of curiosity, I glanced at the price tag of a short gold gown. It stood out like a Quinn in a sea of Darias. The dress was cute and flirty – not my style, but still a pretty choice.

"Four hundred dollars?" I said in shock. "I thought it might be cheaper because it was above the knee. They didn't even have to use that much fabric."

Davy was my perennial emotional support person. "That dress is ugly, anyway. Let me look."

He disappeared into the middle of a rack, like a kindergartener hiding from his mother.

"What are you doing?"

"I just like it in here," he said.

"Weirdo."

Davy thrust his arm towards me from the center of the rack. In his hands was a black dress.

"What about this one?"

"Not bad," I said, holding up the simple stretchy column dress, which was sleeveless with a tie-back. Not my style, either. I checked the price. "One ninety-nine. We're getting better."

"Is it your size?" Davy asked.

I looked. Size 16. "No way. I'd look like a condom full of lard in this thing."

"I've not seen anything past a size 16."

Of course not. "I guess Proffitt's expects girls like me to just cut a head hole in a big tablecloth and belt it. Maybe I should do that. I can use my dress to wipe my mouth, too, after I stuff it with all those pre-prom pizzas."

Davy's arm shot back out and retrieved the black dress.

I flipped through another rack impatiently.

"No. No. Oh, *hell* no. Maybe."

The more I looked around, the more unhappy I became. When I thought of prom dresses, I thought of starched, bell-shaped fabric lined with tulle and deliberately detailed. I thought of glamour. I wanted to be suffocated by sequins and replete with ruffles.

"You know, I don't like any of these dresses. They're all too cutesy or too plain."

"Most of these designs are like, fancy grunge. You could wear a flannel shirt on top of them, and no one would know it's a prom dress," said Davy.

"Prom is the one day of my life I would prefer not to look like I live in a trailer with no air-conditioning," I told him. "I always envisioned myself wearing something fabulous, even if I am fat."

"There are other stores," Davy said. "You wanna go to the food court and regroup? We can get something to drink."

"Sure," I said, and we left Proffitt's behind.

We got a couple of Hint-of-Orange iced teas from Petro's and made our way down to the other end of the mall.

"Do you want to spend the night this weekend?" I asked him. "I think Frances is staying, too. Mom said she didn't care."

Frances was Sissy's best friend and also part of the family. She was at our house as much as Davy was. Mom would let as many friends as we wanted to spend the night, as long as they didn't mind eating cafeteria leftovers for breakfast, lunch, and dinner. Mom's only rule was that no boys were allowed to sleep in our rooms; they had to sleep on the couch.

"I think I'll skip it for a while," said Davy. "Your mom

woke me up at 7 am last time and made me work a jigsaw puzzle with her."

"Yeah, she's really into those puzzles."

"I opened my eyes for five seconds, and she caught me. She started making coffee after that."

On the morning in question, I had slept until 9:30 and awoke refreshed and ready for cafeteria corn dogs. "Did you get the corners done, at least?"

"Shut up."

We didn't have any better luck at JCPenney or Dillard's. Most of the dresses were the same kind of simple, subdued crepe columns we'd seen at Proffitt's. The ones that weren't were shorter and more playful, but equally unflattering. None of them were my size.

We found ourselves in front of Sears.

"Here we are," I told Davy. "The last bastion of hip clothing."

"You're being sarcastic...right?" said Davy, looking at me worriedly.

"Of course, I am."

Shopping at Sears was like hanging out with a friend who was nice enough but, ultimately, a poser. They could never understand why a fresh-off-the-rack flannel shirt and $20 velvet choker would never be as cool as a thrift store find with faded armpits worn underneath a necklace with missing rhinestones.

But here we were. Davy and I made our way to the prom dresses, which were at the back of the store. We didn't detour along the way because there was nothing of interest to slow us down.

Sears' prom selection was by far the smallest. Their dresses were lit from above by harsh fluorescents, like criminals in a lineup.

An unadorned sign reading, *"PROM TIME!"* hung from the ceiling. "Ugh!" I said. "This is the place where dreams come to die."

I unenthusiastically began to flip through their stock. Davy took the rack opposite. After a minute, he spoke up enthusiastically. "Hey, this dress is only a hundred and twenty bucks! And this one's only a hundred and thirty!" He held out a black-and-white gown with an A-line skirt and a smattering of sequins on the bodice.

The dress wasn't tiny, either. "Not bad at all. And the sequins make it look fancier. What size?"

"18."

"Really? I think that might fit."

"Well, go try it on."

I hurried over to the fitting room and closed the door behind me.

"BARF. It smells like sweaty feet in here."

"Just try it on."

I slid off my battered Chuck Taylors and stepped into the dress. I got it mostly zipped up and looked into the mirror expectantly.

The black A-line skirt flattered my hips, but the white top was somehow oversized, making me look puffy.

"What do you think?" asked Davy.

I opened the dressing room door. "I think I look like I was cast as a cloud in an experimental theatre-in-the-round production."

"Yeah. Not good," said Davy.

"I should keep looking."

I redressed in a hurry and shoved my toes into the tops of my shoes, not bothering to tie them.

Davy and I returned to the harshly lit prom corner. "Grab anything that will fit me," I told him.

After scouring the racks completely, we were left with two additional choices.

I locked myself in the fitting room again, kicked my shoes into the corner, and wiggled into a new dress. This one was bluish-purple with a ring of matching embroidered flowers around the neckline.

"Well?"

"The flowers are nice, but the color...I'm not sure."

I walked out of the fitting room and stood in front of Davy.

"You're a bruise!" he said in shock.

"I think it's the lighting."

"I think it's the dress."

"Fine." I headed back in and tried on the other one.

"Uh ... isn't black supposed to be slimming?" I asked Davy from behind the door.

"Let me see it," he said.

I walked out and twirled sarcastically. The heavy, tiered black chiffon skirt rustled noisily with every movement.

"Excuse me, ma'am," said Davy. "Aren't you the crocheted doll in my grandma's bathroom that hides extra toilet paper beneath her skirts?"

I groaned and shuffled back into the fitting room.

"I give up!" I shouted. "I cannot dance to the Quad City DJ's in a wet garbage bag."

I hung the dress back on its inadequate hanger and put on my street clothes. I tied my shoes this time.

"Well, at least I found some dresses that fit me, although I believe I understand now why they were all so inexpensive," I said.

"Maybe they have a better selection at West Town."

"Maybe. But in the meantime, I'm going to go hang these up. And then go on a diet."

"I'm going to the bathroom," said Davy. "I'll be back in a minute."

I returned the dresses to the rack. I walked towards the

bathrooms but stopped in front of the clearance area, my eyes drawn to a messy pile of lustrous fabric. Wait. Were those prom dresses?

They were. I could only assume they were from last season, although they didn't look any different from Sears' current crop of evening wear. There was no point in lying to myself; the choices available to a person my size were as outdated as the Walkman.

On closer inspection, only four gowns were on clearance. Two were size 8, one was size 12, and one was – I tugged the back of the gown to check – size 18.

"Well, okay then," I said. "Let's look at you."

Whoever had put this dress back on the hanger had done a terrible job. Half the dress was hanging on the plastic hanger tab by an inner loop, and the bottom was wrapped over the middle of the hanger like a pair of pants. I carefully unraveled the dress to have a better look.

It was a lovely velvet gown of the deepest blue, with an off-the-shoulder sleeve design and a soft sweetheart neckline. Elegant, timeless, sophisticated. I groped for the price tag. My eyes bugged slightly. And *cheap.*

Davy found me with the dress in my arms, stroking the velvet.

"This was on the clearance rack," I said excitedly. "If it fits, I'm going to get married in it, too."

"It's pretty. How much is it?"

"Seventy-five dollars!"

"No way!"

I returned to the fitting room and stepped into the dress. The skirt was form-fitting like some of the others, but this time, the material had just the right amount of stretch to it. As soon as I pulled the dress up to my waist, I knew it was the one.

I put my back against the mirror and zipped myself up. Then, I turned around.

I was beautiful.

"Oh." A little sound escaped my mouth.

My curves were gently highlighted by the darting of the dress, and the structured sleeves added drama and balance. The midnight blue hue of the gown made my skin glow. Even the freckles on the tops of my shoulders looked like tiny stars instead of sunscreen-less souvenirs of summers past.

I turned to the side. The parts of my arms that made me feel self-conscious were covered, and the velvet hugged my bust, stomach, and backside glamorously.

"*Oh,*" I said again.

"Well?" called Davy from the other side of the door. "What do you think?"

I slowly let the door open on its own.

"I think I'm going to have to buy this dress."

"Wow!" he said. "You look great!"

"Thanks. I feel great. Now I just have to pay for this thing. You got any money? You know we'll pay you back."

"Not enough for a prom dress. What are you going to do?"

"I guess I'll ask them to hold it for me and pray Mom has seventy-five bucks."

I gave the dress to the saleslady.

"How long can you put this on hold?" I asked.

"Twenty-four hours," she said.

"Only twenty-four hours? This is Sears, not Saks," I replied. She gave me a funny look. "I mean, thanks. We'll be back."

After Davy dropped me off, I went straight to Mom's bedroom. She was propped up in bed, reading a library book. Wet bras hung from both bedposts, substituting as a drying rack.

"Hey, guess what!" I said and flopped on the bed next to her, the bras swinging outward with the motion.

"What?"

"I found the perfect prom dress! And it was on clearance. And it was only seventy-five dollars!"

"That's awesome," said Mom. "Where is it?"

"East Towne Sears. I put it on hold tonight, but they can only hold it until tomorrow night. Is there any way we can go buy it tomorrow after school? Please, please, please say we have money."

"Heather, honey, I wish we could, but you know I don't get paid until next week. Would they let you renew the hold? Or maybe put a deposit on it?"

"They don't do layaway with clearance. And I don't know, maybe? But they won't let me keep renewing it for a whole week. Plus, I know if I can't get it now, some other meddling fat girl is going to buy it for sure. It's gorgeous."

"What does it look like?"

"Twilight blue, velvet, form-fitting but flattering." I added in a pitiful voice, "I feel like a movie star with it on."

"Honey, I'm sorry. The best we can do is just hope nobody buys it until next week."

I punched one of the wet bras in frustration. "Gaaaahhhh! All I need is seventy-five freakin' bucks."

"Quit doing that," said Mom.

"Sorry. I'm going to go lay down and be depressed."

"Could you let the dog back in before you do, please?"

On the way to my room, I opened the front door. Cookie ran in, tail wagging. She sniffed my feet. I looked down at her. "Do you have any money?" I asked.

She jumped on the couch without acknowledging my question. Typical.

Since the doorknob to my bedroom had broken off months ago, I could no longer slam my door satisfactorily. Instead, I slid the rock holding it open against the wall behind the door to close it. I had covered the hole where the doorknob used to be with a picture of my favorite actor.

"I really want to look nice at prom, Gary Oldman," I told him.

I climbed into bed, still wearing my clothes, and turned off the light.

↪

THE NEXT DAY AT school, Davy asked me about the dress.

"Did you guys have enough money to buy it?"

"Hell no," I said. "Not until next week."

"Well, maybe it will still be there by then." Davy gave me a watery smile.

"Or maybe a rich old uncle will die and leave us a million dollars, or a psychic will give us winning lottery numbers. Anything can happen if you just believe!" I said. I made a thumbs-down gesture and punctuated it with a long, drawn-out raspberry.

"I'm sorry," said Davy.

"Thanks."

After classes, Davy and I met up as usual. "Do you want to go get a burger and then go watch Sally Jessy Raphael?" he asked me. "My treat."

"Yeah. That sounds nice. I need to tell Mom I'm riding home with you, though. I'll meet you out front."

"Try to grab some cookies or something while you're there."

That boy and his cookies. "Always do," I said.

I wandered into the cafeteria and almost knocked over my petite French teacher, who was holding a Styrofoam cup of iced tea in one hand and a stack of Amsco workbooks in the other.

"Sorry, Madame Stephanie!" I cried. "Close call."

"No worries," she said. "Hey, your mom's looking for you in there." She gestured with her head towards the kitchen.

"I was just on my way to see her. Have a good night."

"See you later!" she said cheerfully. She gave me a little wink.

I walked confidently into the cafeteria kitchen. I knew my way around. The kitchen was kind of cool. Everything in the huge room was covered in stainless steel, and all the cooking implements were oversized. The mixer alone probably weighed 300 pounds.

"Mom?" I called out. "I'm here," I said, my volume fading away on the last word.

Hanging off the pot rack was my prom dress.

"Mama!" I yelled it this time.

She and two other lunchladies, part of the baker's dozen who worked there, walked out of the manager's office where they had been taking a break.

I ran over to her and hugged her hard. "How did you get

my prom dress?!?"

"A couple of us ran over to Sears and got it for you," she said and squished her face next to mine.

"How did you afford it?"

"All the girls chipped in," said Mom.

I looked at the lunchladies, speechless.

"Thank you!" I squealed, hugging them both. "Thank you!"

"You're welcome, honey," one of them said. "Now, you be sure to have a *great time*."

I gave her a kiss on the cheek. "I will."

I ran back over to Mom and to my dress, which had been covered to protect the velvet. The inky blue fabric shone through, glorious even veiled in plastic.

"Isn't it beautiful?" I asked her.

"It really is. Heather, you're gonna be a knockout in this."

"Thanks, Mama."

I plucked the hanger off the pot rack. "I've got to go tell Davy!" I shrieked.

There was no time for cookies. I walked quickly to his car, balancing the hanger hook on my finger. I held the dress away from my body to prevent it from becoming wrinkled.

Davy was jamming out to TLC, eyes closed as he sang.

"Davy!" I yelled, holding my dress in front of me.

His face lit up.

"Is that what I think it is?" he asked.

"The lunchladies bought my prom dress!" I declared happily.

ONCE I HAD THE dress, Davy rented the tux. As promised, he chose a stylish dark blue vest over a single-button shirt with a mandarin collar, forever reppin' the class of '96.

Later that day, I brainstormed with Mom. "Alright," she said to me from across the kitchen table. "Hit me with what else we need to get."

"Okay, there's shoes, a strapless bra, a boutonniere, jewelry, hair, makeup, and a new pair of pantyhose that doesn't have a run in them. Oh, and a nice dinner since Davy's buying the prom tickets."

"Lord, child. Can't y'all just go to Krystal for supper?"

"*Mom.*"

"I know, I know. Look, I don't know how we'll work it out, but we will."

"Maybe I should see if the other lunchladies will adopt me and finish paying for everything else."

"Just pick out cheap stuff, okay?"

"I know, I know," I said.

A week passed. We had made some progress. Two sweet friends at school promised to do my hair, nails, and makeup for free. Plus, Mom found a solution for my fancy dinner.

"One of the coaches at school was selling coupon books for his kid's baseball team. There are a lot of buy-one-get-one-free entrees in there, so I bought one. You can have your pick of the restaurants," she said, dropping it on the coffee table.

"Seriously? You're going to make me use a coupon on prom night?"

"It's either this or chili cheese pups. Sissy and I gotta eat, too."

I exhaled dramatically and flipped through the coupon book. "Hey, these are pretty nice restaurants," I said with relief. "Here's a steakhouse -"

"No steakhouse. Too expensive," interrupted Mom.

I looked through the rest of the coupons silently, carefully tempering my excitement with the reality of Mom's fickle budget. "What about this new French restaurant? Seems like a nice place, but not over-the-top."

A sample menu was printed beside the perforated portion of the coupon. Roasted lamb, lobster and mushroom crepe, seafood bouillabaisse. I knew I wouldn't like any of them, but a French restaurant on prom night sounded very fancy.

I handed her the coupon book. She considered it. "Yeah, y'all can go there. I mean, *oui*."

"Thanks, Mom."

"De nada."

Today was payday, and prom was in two weeks. This was my only shot at the rest of the things I needed.

"So how much money can I spend on shoes and stuff?"

Mom did some quick math in her head.

"Could you buy everything with $100?" she asked.

"I mean... maybe? Davy's boutonniere will be twenty bucks, pantyhose ten, a strapless bra with enough engineering to hoist these babies up without a back injury, thirty."

"We need to get you an 18-hour bra like I wear," Mom replied.

"No, thank you. An 18-hour bra implies that you have to work all day and then only get six hours of sleep at night."

"If that's not womanhood in a nutshell, I don't know what is," said Mom, shaking her head sadly.

"After the bra, that only leaves forty bucks for shoes and jewelry. I don't think that's enough unless, by some miracle, I find those things on clearance."

"Well, you did find your dress on clearance."

"I know. I'm just so tired of making things work instead of just picking what I want."

I found it interesting that my dress had been sloppily thrown on a hanger and rolled up on top of itself. I wondered if God had done that on purpose – disguised my dream dress as unremarkable, keeping it hidden from everyone except the girl who was used to picking through leftovers to try to find treasure. If so, He was a weirdo. I wanted no part of his cosmic gold panning.

I couldn't understand why God's blessings, if that's what this was, often took the form of last-minute rescues or buried fortune. I was no adrenaline junkie. In fact, my nervous system was shot from the constant low-grade stress of being poor. I had no appetite for adventure.

Maybe God was so immense He couldn't understand the finer details of humanity. I wondered if the whole point of sending Jesus and the Holy Spirit was to help Him connect with us better, like kind-hearted union reps meeting with the CEO, advocating for better working conditions on Earth.

At any rate, God was as silent and unreachable to me now as my late father. Memories of better days with either one of them only brought a kind of wistful sadness.

"I understand, baby girl. Believe me, I do."

"I'll make it work, Mom. Thanks."

"You're welcome. Hey, I'm gonna run down to Barbara's house. She invited me over to play gin rummy." Barbara was our new neighbor. She and her husband lived a few trailers down from us. I had only met her once, but she seemed nice.

"Okay, but no bloodshed. She wasn't trained by Mammaw like we were."

Mammaw was a fierce rummy player - scary, even. She was most insistent on winning every game. Over the years, we had learned some questionable strategies and techniques.

"I'll take it easy on her. I want us to be friends."

Mom left. I curled up on the couch with Cookie and put in the VHS tape of Simpsons reruns we had recorded off TV. I pressed play but heard nothing except the sound of Pantera coming from Sissy's bedroom.

Tonight's shoot had begun. Sissy and Frances had been working on a movie for weeks. I didn't quite understand the plot, but I liked their creative chaos. I cheerfully turned up the volume on the TV.

"Teenagers...am I right?" I asked Cookie. She thumped her tail against the couch cushion in reply.

Frances came out of Sissy's room holding a camcorder borrowed from her parents. She was wearing a tinsel wig and a pair of sunglasses with cracked lenses.

"Hey, will you shoot this next scene for us?" she asked. "We both need to be in it."

"Sure," I said.

"Do you have any purple lipstick? I need to draw on my face."

"No, sorry. Just a purple marker."

Frances considered it. "That'll work."

I had no idea what their movie was about, but I couldn't wait to see it.

"Uh...lights, camera, action...and like, stuff," I said in a passable Butthead voice.

"Movies are like...stupid," Frances said in hers.

I turned my attention to their visionary tumult, leaving the rest of the prom problems for a different day.

〜

MOM CAME INTO MY room the next morning carrying a cup of sweet, milky coffee. She did this most school days, and honestly, it was the only reason I could haul myself out of bed and get to class on time.

"Heather Pooh, why don't you get up? Let's talk about prom."

Today was Saturday. I had not planned to emerge from my crypt until much closer to noon.

"Nuhhhhhh!" I made the sound of a tall monster. "I'm still sleeping," I said from underneath my pillow.

"I think you're gonna want to hear this," said Mom. "Now, drink some coffee."

She handed me the cup with my eyes still closed. I took it and guided it into my mouth by pure instinct. The drink was more sugar than coffee, the way I liked it.

"Guess what Barbara wants to do today?"

I slurped half the cup, almost awake enough to engage. "Well, I'm not sure. Did you let her win at rummy last night, or did you go Full Tilt Mammaw on her?"

"Barbara wants to take you to the mall today and buy the rest of the stuff you need."

Mom's words took me by surprise. Hot, sticky coffee

spilled down my arm mid-sip. I hurriedly wiped it off on my black satin bedspread that was purchased long ago from the Fingerhut catalog and paid off in installments.

"Wait, she wants to buy me shoes? And a bra? And jewelry?"

"She said whatever you need. And I think she has a vintage evening bag she'd let you borrow."

I looked at Mom with wonder. "But why would she do that?"

"I told her you were planning your prom night, and we started talking from there. She and her husband don't have any kids. She said they'd be right tickled to help."

The only way Barbara would have found out about my prom needs was if Mom had told her. I remembered Mom's promise that she'd make things work somehow. This was Mama at her best – tenacious, loyal, and insulative. I hadn't felt this protected in a long time.

I was already soggy with knowledge of our family's finances, more saturated than a dripping rum cake. I didn't want to know the details of the conversation between her and Barbara. I was just glad it happened.

"What time are we leaving?" I asked, flinging the covers back excitedly.

~

"Is West Town okay, Heather?" Barbara asked me from the front seat. "It's closer than East Towne and has better parking. That's important for an old fogey like me." I laughed appreciatively. I was on my best behavior. I wanted to be a good investment.

"West Town is great!" I said truthfully. "It's very popular."

"Before we get to the mall, I want to take you to a shoe store I like."

This lady had promised me a small department store's-worth of prom gear. I would have followed her through a swamp full of snakes for free shoes.

"Sounds good to me!"

We pulled into the Bearden Center strip mall. Barbara parked the car in front of our destination.

"Ooh, Heather!" said Mom. "We're going to Coffin Shoes. They're fancy."

"They sound scary."

I had never heard of Coffin Shoes, but their window was full of neat leather selections. Everything on display looked far more expensive than the ratty sneakers I was wearing.

"I have the hardest time finding shoes," said Barbara. "My feet are wide, and the sides of most shoes wear out too fast. Coffin has the most choices, and they're good quality."

I looked at Barbara's kindly face and practical haircut. I liked the idea of buying quality things and taking care of them. I filed the idea away in my aspirational index. Being poor rarely afforded one the choice of spending a little on a throwaway item or spending a lot on something well-made.

You just took your pick from whatever Walmart had and tried to treat it gently so it wouldn't fall apart right away.

We walked into the shoe store. Immediately, a salesman came forward to help.

"How may I help you ladies today?"

I was impressed. I wasn't expecting assistance.

"She's here to look at something for prom," said Barbara.

"How nice!" he said warmly. "What color is your dress? Are you looking for matching shoes? We have heels, flats, and sandals."

"Uh," I said, feeling a little overwhelmed. "My dress is dark blue, and I don't know what I'm looking for. I guess I'll know it if I see it."

"Very good," the salesman said. "Why don't I check back in on you ladies in a bit?"

"Thank you," I said politely.

I turned to Mom and Barbara. "What should I get?" I wondered.

"Why don't you have a look around and see if you like anything?" Barbara asked. "Your mom and I will have a seat."

"Okay." Barbara didn't give me a limit on spending, but she didn't have to. Since she and her husband lived in a trailer, too, I assumed they weren't millionaires. I decided to look for a pair of shoes that I could wear long after prom. This seemed in line with Barbara's philosophy.

I zeroed in on a pair of low-heeled pumps. They were matte black and adorned with large satin bows. I was a fool for bows. Probably every pair of dress shoes I'd owned had been decorated with them, from my first Sunday School sandals to the pair of stretched-out old flats currently living in my closet.

These bows were not styled like a pair of little girls' shoes. They were sophisticated, the edges curling lightly down towards the toe.

"May I try these on, please?" I held up the shoe to the salesman.

"Do you know what size you need, or would you like me to measure your feet?"

I was torn between exposing my sweaty socks and the full experience of an upscale footwear purchase.

Mom spoke up. "Let him measure your feet, Heather Pooh."

I sat down to pull off my shoes and flopped my foot onto the measuring board.

"You're an eight wide," the salesman said. "I'll be back."

He returned in a minute with a box and a handful of those cut-off pantyhose prophylactics designed to protect new shoes from bare soles. I stripped off my socks and stretched a couple over my feet, trying to cover both toes and heels. Impossible.

I stepped into the pumps, pulling up the back of the hose as I did so. The shoes immediately cupped my feet softly. They felt supportive and cushy.

I turned to look at Barbara and Mom in wonder. "These feel *great*," I said. "Are all shoes supposed to feel this way? If so, I have been missing out."

"Your pediatrician told me you were supposed to wear orthopedic shoes when you were little," Mom spoke up, "but we couldn't afford them anymore after Sissy was born. That's why your little toes are so weird. Sorry about that."

Mom's penchant for casual humiliation was legendary. I wonder what Barbara thought of us.

"That explains so much," I said, deadpan.

I took the opportunity to walk around the store for a minute. The shoes were lovely and truly comfortable.

"What do you think?" asked Barbara. "Are those the ones you want to get?"

I panicked. I had forgotten to check the price. What if I had picked the most expensive ones in the store?

"I do. I mean if they're not too expensive."

I checked the sticker. "*Seventy dollars?*" I gasped in shock. I sat back down, resigned to my unattainable tastes, and removed the lovely shoes. Barbara took them from me. She rearranged them neatly in the box.

"They are a little expensive," she said, "but you can wear them with everything. Let's go ring them up."

My mouth hung open in surprise. I had anticipated Barbara's decision-making process perfectly. "Thank you!"

"Barbara, Heather will love wearing those shoes," said Mom. "Thank you."

After she paid, she handed me the slick plastic bag containing my new shoes.

"Next, the mall," Barbara said. "We still have a lot of shopping to do."

We drove up Kingston Pike to West Town and parked at the main entrance. West Town was by far Knoxville's better mall. The stores were always crowded, and today was no exception. Flannelled teenagers were everywhere. Some held hands with their dates, some scowled with intense adolescent emotion while chewing giant slices of pizza, and one stood mesmerized in front of Claire's Boutique.

"Can we look at jewelry first?" I asked. Dozens of rhinestone necklaces lined the shelves, partially visible behind the giant bubble letters of the sign.

"Absolutely. Whatever you like," said Barbara.

"You need something elaborate for that pretty dress," said Mom.

I thought about it. I was already pushing my luck by being fat and trying to look captivating. If my jewelry was too conspicuous, I might skip right past 'majestic' and end up 'Miss Piggy.'

"I think I need something medium-sized. It's got to be big enough to balance out the shoulders but not too gaudy."

"Well, you know a lot more about that than I do," said Mom. "I don't know anything about fashion." On the weekends, when Mom wasn't wearing her lunchlady whites, she was either in stonewashed shorts or a matching sweatsuit, depending on the weather. Sissy, my aunts, and I had given up on trying to teach her the basics of cute clothing.

"You know enough to know I'm right," I said, picking up a jewelry set that caught my eye. The necklace was Y-shaped and smothered with enough rectangular and elliptical rhinestones to outfit an entire Vegas revue. The bracelet and earrings matched the pattern of the necklace. The set was interesting, a little unusual.

"This is what I'm looking for," I told Mom and Barbara. I let the links of the bracelet, the part unattached to the stiff paper backing, rest on my fingers.

Mom and Barbara oohed and aahed. "I really like the shape of the stones," said Barbara. "They remind me of the crown jewels."

"I could start a forest fire with this thing," I said in wonder, casting the stones' reflection all over Claire's. "Barbara, may I please get this set?"

Barbara paused for a moment, mulling over something.

"Yes, you may get it," she said, "but I was thinking. Would you like to borrow my vintage gloves? They would look wonderful with that bracelet."

"Oh my gosh, *yes!*" I cried. "Barbara, thank you so much!"

We took my moderately opulent and moderately priced jewelry set to the register. I never realized how easy elegance could be. All you needed was money and the restraint not to wear anything stonewashed. Now I had the dress, the shoes, the gloves, and the jewelry. I was well on my way to feeling like a princess on the day of prom.

"Why don't we take a break?" asked Mom as we were leaving. "Barbara, lunch is on us today since you're treating Heather to so much."

"Thank you," she said. "What's your favorite restaurant in the food court?"

"Anything but the pizza place." I had very strong opinions about how long the owners parked their pies under heat lamps. "Their stuff tastes reheated even when it's fresh."

"We never have that problem at the cafeteria," said Mom smugly. "Kids love lunchlady pizza."

"We'll pick something else, for sure," said Barbara. "Let's get a bite to eat, and then we'll finish our shopping."

After a meal of 99-cent tacos, we made our way down the other side of the mall.

"Now, let's see," said Barbara. "We still need to buy your underpinnings."

"Yes," I said politely. Her description made underwear sound respectable, but shopping for it was boring. At home, I considered my worn-out bras and snagged pantyhose worthless teammates, all of us thrown together by necessity.

Expecting support from a cheap, old brassiere was futile. Like most group projects I had been a part of, I was used to doing all the heavy lifting.

I wished I hadn't saved the least interesting purchase for last. "Where are we going for that? Proffitt's?" I asked. "I'm not sure if they have my size."

"I was thinking of Lane Bryant," Barbara said.

"What's that?"

"It's a store for ladies of a larger size."

"There's actually a store just for…" I started to say, *fat chicks*, but since I was trying to adopt Barbara's diplomatic demeanor, I stopped myself.

"…larger ladies? Wow."

"Oh, yes," she said. "Their clothes are very stylish."

Mom and I pulled fancy faces at each other. Lane Bryant was news to us.

"How do you know about this place?" I asked. Barbara was a standard size 10, the kind of customer the Misses department relied on to purchase their pastel knit separates.

"My sister likes Lane Bryant," she said. "She lives in the Midwest."

I didn't know what to expect as we strolled in, but it only took seconds for me to feel at home.

The store was cozy but brightly lit. The newest fashions were up front near the window, while the lingerie and jewelry areas were nestled in the back. One of the salespeople was singing along to the local top 40 station playing softly in the background. She was fat and smartly dressed. Two girls, a little older than me, were holding up skirts in front of a mirror, seeing how they looked. They were fat, too. Another salesperson, this one also fat, came out of the back with a rolling rack full of jeans in sizes that would fit us all.

In fact, everyone at Lane Bryant was fat.

And everyone at Lane Bryant looked cute.

"I love it here!" I told my slender fairy godmother. "I never even knew this place existed."

"I'm glad!" said Barbara. "Why don't we take a look around?"

I wound my way around the store, happily stupefied. Everything in the store was available in my size, from casual slip dresses to cool moto jackets to work pants.

"I found Shangri-Lanebryant," I whispered to myself.

I eventually made it to the lingerie section. A row of black beribboned bustiers, sturdy but still pretty, hung upside down off a rack like decorated bats. I looked for my size and found it instantly.

The back of the bustier was held together by a dozen hooks. Its mere existence made the idea of a regular three-hook bra laughable; laughter, of course, that could never be jiggle-free.

"Now, *this* would rein in the girls," I told Mom and Barbara. "And it's on sale!"

"Well, that is right purty," said Mom.

"Can I try it on?" I asked Barbara. "I've never tried on one of these before."

"Of course."

I took my bustier into the dressing room. The dressing room at Lane Bryant didn't smell like feet, unlike Sears. I hung my purse on one of the racks and the garment on the other. After spending a minute opening all those hooks, I placed the bustier around my waist and reattached them. Once the hooks were closed, I tried spinning it around to the other side, like I was used to doing with my regular bra.

The bustier wouldn't move. I tugged it to the right, then to the left, but the stiff, supportive boning didn't allow it. I needed reinforcements.

"Mom!" I called over the door. "Could you come in here, please?"

"What's the matter?"

"I can't button this thing without help."

"Okay. I'm coming in."

I had started over, and now the bustier was in place, though unbuttoned.

"Good Lord," said Mom. "I've seen fewer hooks holding down a tarp in a hurricane."

"We really ask too much of our bra straps," I said.

"Hang on to your girdle, Myrtle," said Mom. "And suck in."

Mom worked quickly. After the first four hooks were fastened, I slowly exhaled, finally confident nothing would pop open and cause injury to innocent bystanders.

"What do you think?"

The bustier had given me the best posture of my life. "It's impossible to slouch in this thing," I told her. "Everything feels locked up tight. No jiggling."

"That's exactly what every mother wants to hear about her teenage daughter."

"Relax, Mom. I couldn't get out of this thing if I tried."

"Is this what you want? If so, I'll go ask Barbara."

"Yes!"

She left, and I looked at myself in the mirror. Wearing good quality things that fit was a remarkable boost to my self-esteem. I wasn't sure what the lesson was here, except that maybe I should skip college and go work for Lane Bryant instead.

After we had decided on the bustier, I quickly picked out a pair of sheer black pantyhose that I knew would fit. I reveled in the feeling of inclusion.

"You know, Barbara," I said as we stood at the wrap stand, "I thought this last stop would be a letdown because we were just buying underwear, but I was wrong."

"Why is that?"

"I guess because this place makes me feel pretty. And normal."

Barbara smiled. The salesperson handed me a printed floral bag full of underpinnings. "Come back and see us," she told me sweetly.

"I will," I promised enthusiastically, now one of Lane Bryant's well-dressed chunky clan. "The future of my spinal health and bosom depends on it. And I didn't even try on any of those cute jackets yet!"

The salesperson nodded confusedly. We waved bye to her.

"Barbara, thank you so much," I said. "This has been an incredible day. Thank you for helping make my prom so special."

"You're welcome, honey," she said. "The pleasure was mine. And I'll give you the gloves and handbag when we get home."

"Thank you again, Barbara," said Mom. "Heather deserves to have only the best." Mom took my hand. "I wish I could give you the world, Pooh."

"I know, Mama."

We returned to the car. "Do you want to play rummy again later?" Mom asked Barbara as we drove away from the mall. "I can bring over my Elvis CD, too."

"That sounds like fun," she said.

"Maybe I'll have better luck tonight," Mom said, winking

at me in the passenger-side mirror. "Last time, I didn't win a single game."

~

I COULDN'T TALK MOM into letting me skip school completely the day of prom. "At least go to first period and take your test about Beowulf," she insisted.

"Do I have to?" I whined. "I really want to sleep in."

"Yes, you have to, but you have my deepest sympathies. That is the most boring poem of all time."

"Agreed," I said, wondering what Beowulf had ever done to her.

"I'll let you take the car home after that, and you can go pick up Davy's boutonniere. I'll get a ride home."

"Mom, did you remember -"

She interrupted me. "Yes, Pooh, I remembered not to smoke inside this morning, so your dress won't smell bad. I smoked outside last night, too."

"Thanks, Mom." She was still trying to quit, but at least my dress wouldn't smell like the Marlboro Man had worn it.

"And I closed all the curtains and turned on the fans, so the house will be as cool as possible when you get dressed. When are your friends coming by to do your hair and makeup?"

"After school. I plan to take a nap and a long shower before they come over."

"Well, be careful driving. I'll be home around then, too.

Don't forget to put Davy's boutonniere in the fridge so the cat won't try to eat it."

Our cat was sweet but dumb. "I will."

I drove to the florist and picked up the boutonniere. They had done a nice job, framing a white rose with greenery and wrapping the wiring with navy blue tape. I stopped by the grocery store and bought a thick deli sandwich for lunch with the change leftover from the florist. I'd need my strength to get ready in case I didn't like anything at the French restaurant. I began to feel excited. We had been scrambling to make things perfect for weeks. Now, we would see the result.

After my lunch, which I shared with Cookie, I stretched out on the couch next to her and took a quick snooze. Mom's diligence in keeping down the heat made the trailer bearable as I showered and washed my hair. I was barely sweating even after using the hair dryer.

My friends Laurel and Rochelle arrived loaded down with makeup and hair tools. Within ninety minutes, my face was glamorously painted, and my hair was curled softly. As a final touch, they added baby's breath to the braid that ran across the top of my head.

Mom got home right as Rochelle was finishing my nails.

"Hi, Mom!" I called, waving both hands wildly.

"Baby girl, you look so pretty! Ladies, you did a wonderful job," said Mom.

"Thank you. Now go put on your dress!" cried Laurel. "Davy will be here any minute."

I went into Mom's bedroom and shut the door. My dress was hanging in her closet. I threw off the old nightgown I had been wearing over my bustier and pantyhose. Carefully, I stepped into the bottom of the dress and pulled it up. I reached around to zip it.

Mom called from the kitchen. "Heather Pooh, do you need any help? Did you get that crazy bra on without straining anything?"

"I'm good!" I called back. For whatever reason, I wanted to finish this by myself. "I'll be out in a minute."

"Okay but hurry up! We all want to see you!"

I pulled my dress up a few inches and slid each foot, one at a time, into my elegant new shoes. When I was finished, I looked down. The refined black satin bows peeked out from under the hem as if to say hi.

I fastened the exquisite necklace and earrings, carefully pulling on my borrowed ivory gloves before adding the bracelet. Despite the animated chatter coming from my friends and Mom in the kitchen, the room felt quiet and tranquil. I stood back from the vanity mirror and observed my reflection.

I was dazzling. The corners of my mouth turned upward in a smile, then a grin. My happiness could not be contained. Was I really this stunning?

"Thank you," I said. It was a prayer of appreciation that included them all - my mother, my friends, our neighbor, and every lunchlady at Karns High School. I begrudgingly acknowledged God, too, for involving Himself in the inconsequential matters of feminine adolescence. He was easiest to love when He felt so close.

From the crown of my curls to the tips of my high heels, my loveliness was the sum total of the women devoted to making this night special. My joyful indebtedness crystallized into a memory as strong and splendid as a diamond, a memory more enduring and endearing than anything else that would happen that night.

Garbed in gratitude, shod in sisterhood, I walked proudly into the kitchen, radiant in my clearance finery.

Their burst of applause said it all.

NOUVEAU RICHE, FOR A WEEK

"I'll have your total in a moment, ma'am," the H&R Block representative told Mom.

"Lord, please let it be enough to fix the bathrooms," Mom said, eyes raised heavenward. My eyes followed hers to the stained, textured tiles of the office's drop ceiling.

"Amen," I said solemnly. Filing taxes was serious business in our family. We relied on Mom's annual income tax return to catch up on bills, major repairs, and brief hedonistic shopping sprees. This year, the rotted bathroom floorboards and cracked plastic bathtubs were of utmost importance.

The representative's long, cabernet-colored fingernails quickly tapped numbers into her adding machine. Her staccato typing was fast and capable, and I held my breath nervously waiting for her answer. She looked trustworthy. Whatever she said would be correct.

Finally, the tapping came to a stop.

I looked at Mom anxiously.

"Alright. Your refund amount is three thousand, two hundred, sixty-eight dollars and sixty-four cents."

Mom shot out of the plastic office chair like a handful of confetti thrown into the air.

"Praise Jesus!" she shouted, holding her hands towards the ceiling in worship. "We can fix the bathrooms!"

Three thousand, two hundred, sixty-eight dollars and sixty-four cents was a staggering amount of money. I was in shock. I was grateful for the hard plastic seat beneath me, afraid my legs would give out if I stood up too quickly.

"Are you serious?" I asked the representative.

"Umm…yes?" she said, slightly nervous from the amount of Mom's energy bouncing around the small room.

"That's. Frickin. *Awesome!*" I added. Tax time was the only time being poor seemed to have any advantages. I didn't understand that all we'd really done was hand Uncle Sam an interest-free loan with Mom's hard-earned money.

The H&R Block lady tried to get things back on track. "If we file today, you should receive your refund by mail in about six to eight weeks. Or, if you'd like to pay a small fee, we can send your refund to your bank electronically, and you'll receive it in seventy-two hours."

Mom returned to her chair. "How small a fee?"

"For a refund your size…one hundred and nineteen dollars."

A hundred and nineteen dollars was more than a small fee. I could see Mom trying to decide whether we could survive another six to eight weeks straddling the cracks in the bathtubs while we showered. There was nothing holding the middle of the bathtubs together anymore except hope.

I spoke up helpfully.

"I can't handle another two months of sitting on a leaning toilet. If I fall through the floor and die from being impaled on a tank shard, I'll miss my chance to be commencement speaker."

The representative's eyes bugged slightly upon hearing this pronouncement. "Plus, if you get the money early, we can actually afford to buy my graduation announcements and all that," I said.

That was all the convincing Mom needed. "Okay. We'll pay to get the money faster."

Somewhere, H and R Block high-fived each other.

"Yes!" I said, pumping my arm triumphantly. A new, lump-free bathroom was only days away.

～

SEVENTY-TWO HOURS LATER, I woke up before my alarm clock and sat up in bed eagerly. The sooner I started getting ready for school, the sooner I'd be home, and the sooner we could talk about all that money.

I pranced into the kitchen after hastily dressing. Mom, always an early riser, was already sitting at the kitchen table with her cup of coffee. From Sissy's room, I heard the jingle of Cookie's collar as she jumped down from Sissy's bed. They were awake, too.

The cordless phone sat next to Mom's cup of coffee. Underneath it was her checkbook.

"So?" I asked Mom. "Did we get it yet?"

"Yep. I just called the automated bank line."

"Woo hoo! When are we going to get the floors fixed?"

"I'm going to talk to ole Pookiedoo at school. He knows someone who does construction." *Pookiedoo* was the word Mom used when she couldn't remember someone's name.

"Who's Pookiedoo? I hope he knows what he's talking about."

Mom scoffed. "You know…ole Pookiedoo. The one who has them old cars. His wife teaches hairdos down at the vocational school."

I knew exactly who she was talking about. Pookiedoo was a football coach who liked to restore vintage Chevys. He was married to the cosmetology teacher.

"No. I don't know which Pookiedoo you're talking about. Do you mean the wrestling coach?"

"No."

"The secretary's husband?"

"No."

"The school security guard? I thought he was into salsa dancing, not cars."

"*No*," Mom said, finally realizing I was teasing her. "Shit fire, Heather. It's ole Pookiedoo. You know who I'm talking about."

I started laughing.

She playfully swatted me with the checkbook. "Ha ha, punkinhead. Go finish getting ready for school."

After school, Davy and I ran errands for our theatre class. When he dropped me off at home, a man in a truck was pulling out of the driveway. I went inside to find Mom.

"Was that ole Pookiedoo's friend?" I asked.

"It was. Guess how much it's gonna cost to fix everything?"

"How much?" I prayed Mom wasn't teeing up an anecdote that ended with her signing up for loan financing.

"Just $1,200!"

I collapsed onto the couch in relief. "Oh, thank God!" Knowing we would once again be able to stand directly under the showerhead without fear and still afford to wash our hair with the best drugstore shampoo available made me feel like a millionaire.

"What are we going to do with the rest of the money, then? Can I get my graduation stuff?"

"Yes. You can get your announcements and your cap and

gown. And since you're speaking at graduation, you can get a new dress, too."

I was only selected to be a speaker because just three of us tried out. Speaking at commencement had always been a goal of mine. Every movie with a graduation scene made it clear that the speaker was the smartest person in the class. In reality, twelve years of being a good student hadn't been nearly as important as simply writing a speech the night before and showing up early to audition. Even so, I was proud of myself.

"Thanks, but I don't want a new dress," I told Mom. "It'll just be covered up all day by my big blue gown. What does Sissy want?"

"Sissy wants a guitar. I told her she could get one."

Guitars were cool. I loved singing with Sissy, although I was no good at harmony. I just picked a note above the one Sissy sang and tried to make it work. The only reason we sounded good together on "Delta Dawn" was because she let me have the melody.

"Maybe I should get a guitar, too. It might help my singing," I said hopefully.

"Whatever you girls want. I think we all need a little treat."

"What about some new clothes? And a new purse? And could I get some lipstick from the mall?"

Mom held up her hand. "Slow down, baby girl. I think so, but I want to try to save a little bit, too."

"I'm sorry. I'm just so excited!" I said.

"I am, too. In fact, I'm gonna take you girls to a fancy restaurant tonight. I've still got the coupon book you used for prom."

My mind was spinning with possibilities. "That sounds amazing!"

Mom took the coupon book from the cabinet and handed it to me. "I'm gonna ask Sissy where she might want to go," said Mom.

Cookie was next to me on the couch. I reached over and mushed her soft beagle ear happily. "Get ready," I told her. "We're going to bring you back some awesome leftovers. Maybe an entire steak."

"We're not bringing home an entire steak for the dog!" Mom called from Sissy's room.

After much discussion and a thorough perusing of the coupons, we decided on Grady's. We knew it by reputation only.

Grady's Goodtimes was as quintessentially Knoxville as the Sunsphere or the Vols and was hugely popular with young professionals in the 1980s. The food was tasty but unpretentious, the atmosphere upbeat, and the drinks top shelf.

That evening, we walked in like we owned the place and were seated immediately.

"Thank you," I said to the server, who handed me a thick menu in a laminated jacket. I opened it. The edges were sticky.

I fanned it out on the table and glanced around, wanting to take in the full experience. I was disappointed with what I saw. Although the lights were dimmed, it was obvious the restaurant's interior was frozen in time.

Grady's used to be cool. Not anymore. Now, it was the kind of place former fraternity and sorority royalty might bring their kids for lunch after Sunday worship, desperately nostalgic for the taste of Screwdrivers mixed with strawberry lip gloss. I could only assume their eyes were able to look past the faded wallpaper and scarred bar-tops in a way I couldn't. I wonder what it felt like to peak right after college. I felt sorry for these tarnished kings and queens.

I wiped my tacky fingers along the top of my skirt. "Wow. I'm glad Davy and I didn't come here before prom," I said. "What happened to this place?"

"I don't know," said Mom, "but we can still have a good time. Maybe the food is still worth eating."

"I hope so." The French restaurant I had chosen for prom had been a disappointment, too, full of oversauced items and tiny bistro tables that left no room for forearms or purses.

Sissy, Mom, and I placed our orders. We immediately began to talk about the new bathrooms. "When can the guy start?" I asked Mom.

"He's going to start this weekend and fix one at a time.

That way, we can still use one bathroom while he's working on the other."

"How's he going to prevent the same thing from happening in the future?"

"He said he's going to add extra support under the trailer."

"We could all use some extra support."

Mom and Sissy ate their side salads quietly as I launched into a monologue about my friends' college plans. "And then said he might go to Pellissippi Community College instead because it's cheaper, but I think it's really because he's secretly a Florida Gators fan," I finished. I finally took a bite of my salad. "Blech! Does this have sardines in it?" I asked, horrified.

"I think it's anchovies," said Mom.

"Who puts anchovies in a garden salad? Is this a restaurant for cats?"

"Oh, Heather Pooh. It's not so bad. Here, I'll eat it," said Mom, reaching across the table for my plate. She took another bite. "Meow."

I decided not to comment on my mother's feline palate. "Well, maybe the entrées will be better."

They weren't. Sissy's pasta was wilted and lukewarm, and Mom's burger was cold.

"These chicken tenders are so dry they're making my teeth squeak. I think we should send all this food back," I said. I looked around for the server, but he was nowhere to be found.

Mom pushed the rest of her burger away. "Why bother? You think they're gonna suddenly know how to cook just because we reorder everything?"

"I wish someone would have warned us before we spent all this money, that's all."

"Hey baby, don't forget. We've got a *coupon*. The joke's on them."

"Well, it is called Grady's Goodtimes, not Grady's Goodfood," I said, and we all cracked up.

The server finally reemerged, reeking of cigarette smoke. "May I interest you in dessert? What about a slice of our famous chocolate bar cake?"

"No," we said in unison.

"Just the check, then."

He brought it over to us. I reviewed the charges to make sure our coupon had been applied. I noticed an emblem on the bottom of the paper. I recognized it as the logo of a national chain restaurant.

"Hey!" I said, "no wonder this place stinks now. Grady's must have gotten bought out by some big corporation. That explains a lot. I guess they figured rubes like us wouldn't know the difference, or maybe they have a secret Grady's in the back for rich people." I was miffed to have been robbed of yet another fancy restaurant experience.

"We *are* rich," said Mom, "at least for a while. But if that's the case, then I'm glad we didn't send back the food. They probably would have just fished another plastic bag of burger meat out of a cooler and tossed it in the microwave. We're still going to leave a good tip for the waiter, though. It's not his fault everything tasted like prison food."

"How do you know what prison food tastes like?" I wondered.

"There's a lot you don't know about me, punkinhead."

"Well, the night is still young. Perhaps we can order non-fancy pizza later."

"Where do y'all girls want to go next?"

"I'd like to go to Walmart or Kmart or something. I want a new purse and stuff."

"Not the mall?"

"Nah. We'll get more for our money away from the mall. Let's try not to get ripped off twice in two hours."

"That sound good? You ready to go?" Mom asked Sissy, who kept her face expressionless but gave a double thumbs up, like Fonzie. We cracked up again.

"I wished our dinner would have been better," I said with disappointment. "I wanted this to be a celebration since I'm getting so close to graduation."

"This can still be a celebration," said Mom, picking up her sweating glass of cola. "We can have a toast."

Sissy and I played along, holding up our almost empty glasses of raspberry iced tea and gesturing grandly.

"To Heather, my firstborn, who, despite tough times, tough chicken fingers, and almost falling through the floor of the trailer, managed to kick butt in high school and who will do the same in college. I love you, Pooh, and I'm proud of you. Your daddy would be, too."

We clinked Grady's dull and worn glass tumblers together.

"Thanks, Mama."

"And thank you, Jesus, for taking care of us," she added, lifting her soda high so He could take a supernatural sip. Sissy and I nodded respectfully and tilted our glasses toward hers.

"One more," I said. "A toast to us for holding on tight to this ridiculous roller coaster of existence. If I have to drive through life stuck in a clown car, I'm glad y'all are riding shotgun." We clinked glasses again, this time sucking our straws noisily to catch the remaining dribbles of our drinks.

"Now, let us dash to the store before we run out of money, for we will be poor again soon," Mom said in a swashbuckling voice. "But tonight, we will live like Vanderbilts, like Waltons, like Rockefellers!"

"Hang on a minute!" I pretended to be serious. "We may not be poor forever. Things can only get better, right?"

The three of us left the restaurant still laughing.

1994

NATIONAL HONOR SOCIETY INDUCTION – 1995

1996

OFFICIAL PÖR CLUB PORTRAIT 1996

AUTHOR BIO

HEATHER REAM'S FIERCE DESIRE to find common ground has led her to poke around the most tender, and personal, truths of what it means to be human. Heather is a Christ follower and the proud owner of a twangy Appalachian accent. She lives with her husband in Knoxville, TN.

heatherream.com

www.ingramcontent.com/pod-product-compliance
Lightning Source LLC
Chambersburg PA
CBHW030405130626
46549CB00004B/1645